HAUNTED
ANTRIM

HAUNTED
ANTRIM

Madeline McCully

Madeline McCully

The
History
Press
Ireland

I dedicate this book to my children

First published 2017

The History Press Ireland
50 City Quay
Dublin 2
Ireland
www.thehistorypress.ie

© Madeline McCully, 2017

The right of Madeline McCully to be identified as the Author
of this work has been asserted in accordance with the
Copyright, Designs and Patents Act 1988.

British Library Cataloguing in Publication Data.
A catalogue record for this book is available from the British Library.

ISBN 978 0 7509 8360 0

Typesetting and origination by The History Press
Printed and bound by CPI Group

CONTENTS

FOREWORD

I was delighted to be asked to write the foreword for *Haunted Antrim*, since that is my home county.

I was born in Ballymena, the 'middle town' of County Antrim, and in my early years there was no television so there was a lot of talking in our house. I listened to stories around the kitchen table and many of these tales concerned ghostly apparitions and haunted places. Sure, didn't my own eldest brother, Bill, see and hear a wailing banshee the night before a death? He believed that till the day he died.

Wide-eyed and open-mouthed, I heard the stories about Galgorm Castle, located not a mile from my home. Even as a young child, I knew all about the locked room where Dr Colville reputedly sold his soul to the devil. Is it any wonder then that I grew up to be a storyteller with a liking for spooky tales?

In this collection, storyteller Madeline McCully has gathered together some of my favourite ghost stories from places that I know very well. Apart from my own background knowledge, people who live near particular locations have corroborated many of the tales.

For example, a classroom assistant in north Belfast once told me about hearing the hoof-beats of Galloper Thompson's horse as he clattered around streets near her home. An old man in Randalstown told me all about the banshee of the O'Neills. Go to Rathlin Island and folk there can still recount the story of the dreadful massacre when many women and children were butchered by troops led by the Earl of Essex, under the orders of Sir Francis Drake and other English noblemen. It is said that from the mainland near Ballycastle, Sorley Boy McDonnell was seen 'to run mad with sorrow' as he watched the women and children he had sent to the sanctuary of the island being brutally butchered. They say their cries can still be heard on Rathlin and there was talk of retribution when HMS *Drake* was sunk just off the island in Church Bay by a German U-boat in 1917.

In these pages you will find characters such as Squire O'Hara, who rides out on Christmas Eve at Crebilly outside Ballymena, the White Lady, who haunts Antrim Castle, and the poor demented Lady Isabella, gazing out to sea from her tower at Ballygally Castle.

County Antrim has many places where every stone could tell a story. It would take a brave person to explore Dundermot Mound near Glarryford, one of two 'Gateways to Hell', a ghostly portal to the other world. Or indeed to tread on the stone steps at Bonamargy Friary outside Ballycastle, under which lies the body of the Black Nun, Julia McQuillan, who was famed for her predictions.

In her collection, Madeline provides intriguing titbits to lure readers into further investigation. She whets the appetite and shares intriguing evidence. Readers and listeners have an enduring thirst for this type of tale and the easy style of the writing will lead them to further explore this popular genre.

The telling of ghost stories is still flourishing in County Antrim, which now boasts its own Ghosts in the Glens Storytelling Festival every October. At the festival, listeners can learn more about frightening apparitions such as the Witch of Glentow or the Wraith of Rathlin, whom they meet here in these pages.

Sceptics may doubt the veracity of some of the stories, but I can vouchsafe that when I am out telling ghost stories, I always come home with more stories than I tell as listeners queue up to share their own experiences with me.

Reading Madeline McCully's *Haunted Antrim* will give readers the chance to become better acquainted with some of the special places in my native county. I leave it up to the reader to decide what is true and what is not.

All I know is that when a sceptic asks me why I believe in the existence of such things as fairies or ghosts, I simply reply 'because they exist'.

Liz Weir
Storyteller, writer and listener
2017

ACKNOWLEDGEMENTS

I have thoroughly enjoyed researching and writing the stories in this book. The Antrim coast is a favourite place of mine and over the years we have brought many visitors to the area to admire its majestic scenery and to share with them the myths and legends of this part of Ulster.

My husband Thomas has kept me focused throughout. He seemed to know instinctively when to bring cups of tea and put meals on the table during the writing process. He has driven me around and made each journey memorable and reminded of the importance of laughter.

In researching I have discovered more haunted places than I can include in this book. I must acknowledge the people who have shared their stories with me, in particular Jim McNeill, Thomas Robinson and Heather Barkley.

Ken McCormack's help was invaluable. Ken is a collector, broadcaster, writer and a great storyteller in his own right. I thank him for his total availability when I needed help or clarification. Nothing was too much trouble for him including proofreading the final manuscript and I am extremely grateful. He was encouraging and supportive all the way.

Libraries N.I were unbelievably helpful – especially Linda Ming and Maura Craig of Derry Central Library who were always on hand to help with the research. The library is almost my second home.

I am grateful to the staff of Belfast Central Library who found suitable books for me and the Linen Hall Library who welcomed me, supplied information and books and a relaxed space in which to read them. Noreen Mullan of the Braid and Mid-Antrim Museum was most helpful and kind.

A very big thank you to Jim McCallion who gave me much needed help in preparing the photographs for the book. It is difficult to access photographs of times gone by but he was patient and always helpful when I asked for help.

I want to acknowledge information received from Joe Baker of the Glenravel History Project and Joe Grahame of *Rushlight* magazine.

I owe a debt of gratitude to Liz Weir, one of the world's greatest storytellers. She runs various storytelling and musical events in her Ballyeamon barn. Thank you, Liz, for your encouragement and practical help in bringing this book to the public.

Over the years the Arts Council Northern Ireland have been generous in their awards for gathering and researching folklore. Without their help I couldn't have continued to preserve these stories.

Finally, I would like to acknowledge The History Press's editors, Beth Amphlett and Andrew Latimer, for their help in preparing the manuscript.

Many of those who contributed information wished to remain anonymous and I respect that. Therefore I will thank all of you at once for taking the time to tell me the stories and allowing me to use them. I hope that I have done them justice.

The long canal, Antrim Castle. (Photo L. Shepperd)

INTRODUCTION

For the olden memories fast are flying
    from us;
Oh, that some kind hand would come
    and bind them in a garland
Ere the present hardens and the past
    grows cold and dumb.
            Sam Henry, *Songs of the People*

WHEN I hear a ghost story I am right back in my great-aunt's little cottage in Donegal, with my ear pressed against the door of the lower bedroom, listening to the murmur of voices in the kitchen. How I would have loved to be among the men and women listening to their stories. But maybe the fact that we children were sent off to bed made me want to hear more and learn more about the ghosts and fairies who seemed to haunt the lonely roads and dark hills.

The cottage was without running water and electricity and two candles on saucers lit the bedroom. In their meagre light ghostly shadows flickered on the walls and the coats hanging on hooks looked like ghosts ready to emerge out of the gloom. When the thrill of being frightened became too much it was time to dive into the big iron bed and snuggle under the bedclothes, say my prayers and sink into sleep thinking of ghosts and goblins.

After the holidays back at home some of my friends had televisions in their houses but until I was 12 we didn't. It was probably the best thing that could have happened because at night before we went to bed we took our supper in the firelight and my mother would often tell us stories that might not otherwise have been told.

My mother was born in Donegal and the cottage and the hills were our playground when the holidays came around. We heard stories that had been handed down from her parents and grandparents and it was as if the people and places she spoke of were still around.

In hindsight, I wish that I had asked more questions and listened more. But that early experience made me curious enough to gather stories and record them because although technology is wonderful we are in danger of losing the magic of storytelling.

I meet very interesting people as I travel around, and I've discovered that everyone has a story to tell. For the purposes of this book, however, I have had to confine myself to the haunted stories of County Antrim and the part of Belfast City which is in that county.

Many of the stories are based on tragedies of bygone times but I have included modern ones because the time for ghosts is not yet past. One story I heard several years ago when visiting the Glens of Antrim was the story of the ABC Theatre in Belfast. The story stuck in my mind and when I decided to include it I discovered that Jim MacNeill lived in Canada. He kindly talked to me several times on the phone and his words were so powerful I thought what better than to let him tell it himself.

When I hear about the presence of a ghost I want to research what is behind the story. I want to know the what, when, where, how and why. Often people would say that the appearance of a ghost goes back to a tragic event, or a warning of imminent danger or perhaps the person has left some unfinished business on earth, as in the old woman in the cow-herder's story. Sometimes it is the appearance of a 'wraith' warning of a death as in the Rathlin story. The Banshee is one of the common apparitions of Celtic culture, a female creature who portends a death to come but that also serves to remind us of the dead by her recurring appearances.

The list of apparitions goes on, as do the mysteries – perhaps that is why ghost stories are such a source of endless fascination, particularly if we know the place where they take place and the history behind them.

Drawing on a mix of historical and contemporary sources, I hope this book will fascinate anyone with an appetite for the unexplained.

Antrim Castle.

1

EERIE CASTLES

The Ghosts of Antrim Castle

> Fear came upon me, and trembling, which made all my bones to shake. Then a spirit passed before my face; the hair of my flesh stood up.
>
> *The Book of Job 4:14-15*

A ghostly presence is said to stalk the grounds of Antrim Castle. The unhappy apparition is believed to be the ghost of a young local girl called Ethel Gilligan, a servant girl working for the family at the castle at the time of an arson attack. Locals saw the blazing building and one man ran with a ladder and climbed to the window of the servants' quarters to rescue Ethel. Although she wasn't burnt, she later died of smoke inhalation. It seems that her spirit wanders close to the place where she was laid on the ground after her rescue and where she took her last breath. The locals refer to her ghost as the 'White Lady'.

Antrim Castle had an eventful history during its 309 years. Sir Hugh Clotworthy, an Englishman of the planter class, was raised to the peerage by patent under Charles II and given the title of Baron of Lough Neagh and Viscount of Massereene. He oversaw the building of the castle in 1613 on the beautiful banks of the Six Mile Water River beside the lough. When his son, Sir John Clotworthy, inherited the title of Viscount Massereene, he set about extending the castle in 1662 or thereabouts.

The Stone Wolfhound and companion.

The Jacobite general Richard Hamilton raided the castle in the 1680s and gave his men the freedom to take whatever they wished as payment for their services to the king. They ran wildly through its corridors and rooms and looted the castle's treasures of silver plate and furniture worth more than £3,000. Not content with that, they damaged much of what could not be removed.

Antrim Castle was rebuilt in 1813 as a three-storey Georgian-Gothic castellated mansion, designed by Dublin architect John Bowden. The seventeenth-century formal garden added at that time was a showpiece in Ulster, featuring a long canal with another canal at right angles to it. To complete the design, a moat reminiscent of that of a Norman castle was added.

The Massereene family took up residence again and Lord and Lady Massereene were hosting a grand ball in the castle on 28 October 1922 when an IRA gang allegedly set fire to it – apparently on information received from a servant who was thought to be a republican sympathiser.

The daughter of the Archbishop of Armagh, the Most Rev. Charles D'Arcy, who was staying there for the ball, was persuaded by a mysterious white-robed figure of a woman to jump out of a window to save herself.

The ghost of the 'White Lady' was seen walking in the gardens and amidst the ruins of the castle before its demolition in 1970. But this has not been the only paranormal activity on the grounds. Apparently, in former times a coach pulled by six black horses galloped towards the castle, but when it reached a deep pond, it sank, causing the death of all of those on board. On that anniversary each May the fearful whinnies of the animals accompanied by the screams of the drowning travellers disturb the night.

Yet another ghost story concerns Lady Marian Langford, daughter of Sir Roger Langford of Muckamore, who was engaged to Sir Hugh Clotworthy. Lady Marian was taking a stroll along the water's edge when she was startled by a deep growl behind her. Upon turning round, she was faced with the horrifying sight of a wolf baring its teeth and ready to pounce. Lady Marian fell in a dead faint and when she came to she saw the bloodied body of the dead wolf and felt her hand being licked. Lying beside her was a wounded wolfhound, which in defending her had suffered injury. Lady Marian took him to Antrim Castle and tended his wounds but shortly afterwards the wolfhound mysteriously disappeared.

It is believed, though, that some years later the deep baying of a wolfhound was heard above the storm and this warned of an imminent attack by the enemy. A single cannon shot from 'Roaring Tatty', as the gun was called, was enough to repel the attack and at dawn a stone wolfhound was seen by the gateway.

It is said that this stone wolfhound will safeguard the Clotworthy family name so long as it is not removed. Legend also has it that this was once the flesh-and-blood animal that saved Lady Marian.

Spookily enough, those who walk through the gardens are often mystified by the sound of heavy breathing, not unlike that of a dog panting.

The Haunting of Glenarm Castle

Glenarm Castle, built in 1636, stands 'like the enchanted keep of a fairy tale … It became the residence of the McDonnells – Earls of Antrim – after the accident of Dunluce Castle compelled a removal to some safer spot.' (*Hall's Ireland*).

It is situated in a beautiful area of parkland and forest within sight and sound of the sea and it is the last place one would expect to find a haunted castle. But haunted it is, and the background story lies in its violent history.

After the Ulster Land War of the 1770s, Lord Antrim was governor of the county. He ruthlessly evicted his tenants from his demesne, leaving bitterness in the hearts of the people and, as one would expect, a desire for revenge. Lord Antrim feared for his life and travelled to Dublin to beg the lord lieutenant for a company of soldiers to accompany him to Glenarm.

On his return in the first week of February, he sat down to supper and for some unknown reason he first placed an unframed portrait of his mother-in-law, the late Lady Meredyth, on the sideboard. A shot, likely intended for him, was fired through the window and struck the portrait of the woman on the shoulder.

It must be said that another attempt was made, but that the assassin mistook young Lieutenant Walsh for Lord Antrim and shot him as he returned to Ballymena after visiting Glenarm Castle. The assassin probably saw the escort of two soldiers and assumed that it was the earl. Lord Antrim escaped further attacks on his life and died of natural causes in 1721.

About the year 1853, a later Lord Antrim was reminiscing with a friend about the shot portrait. The friend (referred to only as 'LLA') asked to see it and Lady Antrim, who was also present, point-blank refused to accompany him to the room where the old portrait had been left. She bade her husband to stay with her and directed the friend upstairs.

'Turn right to a short passage and go into the third door,' said she.

Glenarm Castle.

The room was small with little or no furniture and the only light came from a tiny window without a curtain. The visitor saw the portrait and wasn't impressed. He described it later as 'a mere daub of a very commonplace woman with a blue dress, a pearl necklace and a gold comb.'

The man crossed to the window to look out and when he faced the room again he was astounded to see a woman standing in the doorway. At first he thought that it was his imagination because daylight was fading fast, but to his alarm she stared fixedly at him with dark deep-set eyes. She was tall and in the short time that he looked he could see that she was wearing a petticoat of blue and brown homespun material and added, 'Her arm was extended holding the string of a cap with frills such as Irishwomen used to wear'.

The visitor assumed she was one of the maids who had followed him upstairs to check what he was doing in the upper rooms. He passed her in the doorway and returned downstairs to Lord and Lady Antrim and thought no more about the incident. In June 1855, the aforementioned LLA and his father entertained a Captain Orlebar, a naval friend, who had spent a night in Glenarm Castle as the guest of Lord Antrim. During the conversation, he spoke of the earl's failing health and mentioned what he called 'a serious personal incident in his night there'.

'I was awakened very early by the birds singing in the trees close to the window,' he said. 'It was bright daylight and I turned on my elbow to reach for my watch from a small table where my candle stood, and there, right in the doorway, was a woman, evidently a servant. By her dress she had just risen for she wore a mobcap and was holding the strings out

Portrait of Lady Meredyth.

in a dazed manner with bare arms.

'"Well," I cried sharply and she vanished. I did not say anything about this at breakfast but by Jove, I thought it was perhaps some sort of funny Irish way of seeing if their guests were still alive.'

Soon after Captain Orlebar's visit, LLA went to see the MacDonnell in Glenarriff who at this time was very old and feeble but still retained a clear memory of the past. The old man enjoyed sharing stories, especially those of local legends and 'auld warl cracks'.

'Tell me,' said LLA, 'were there ever any ghosts in Glenarm Castle?'

'Oh aye, plenty, you may be sure,' was his answer. 'Why, Ann Bisset walks there to this day and strange to say, it is only to strangers she ever appears, for she would never ask a favour of us, for we McDonnells are her sworn enemies.'

This convinced LLA that there was indeed a ghost in the castle and that he had seen it. But further proof was to come. In 1856, after the old earl had died,

The Ghost of Ann Bisset.

the new lord was due to take up residence. He ordered many alterations to the castle to accommodate his large family, and in his absence the local police officer, de Gernon, kept a watch on the place. He invited LLA to come see the changes that had been made, and as they approached the castle de Gernon explained that a few days previously he had been called to go there because the men who were clearing out the moat had found a skeleton under some of the stones which had moved during the work.

De Gernon had no doubt that the skeleton was one of the household or family of Bisset, who had probably been killed, a raid, perhaps more suspiciously had been murdered by one of the MacDonnells. Later the bones were interred in the old graveyard, which is now covered and is ploughed land.

Although this took place in the nineteenth century, the ghost is still believed

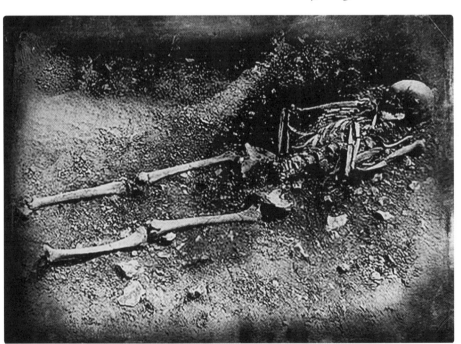

Skeletal remains found at Glenarm Castle in 1856 during renovations. They were believed to be the remains of Ann Bisset.

Galgorm Castle.

to appear near or in the guest rooms of the castle dressed in the same garb described by Captain Orlebar and LLA. Those who saw it explained that she was so real they simply took her as a servant dressed in old-fashioned garb.

In the 1990s, the *Belfast Telegraph* interviewed Hector McDonnell, who grew up in Glenarm Castle and stated: 'The paranormal activity was so pronounced that my mother had every room in the castle exorcised, except for the attic.'

He went on to explain that at the age of 12 he was sent to investigate the terrible stamping noise coming from the attic and had a terrifying experience. He said that he turned on the lights to the attic at the bottom of the stairs but when he reached the room the lights went off and he was left in the dark. Hector had an awful sense of foreboding that whoever turned off the lights was right behind him and he ran back down the stairs as fast as his legs could carry him.

The noises continued for the next fifteen years and the only explanation is that the spirit of whoever was murdered fled to the attic when the house was exorcised.

The 6th Earl of Antrim petitioned Rutland, the lord lieutenant, that his title might descend to his daughter Anne, in the absence of a male heir, and this was granted. Her daughter Frances Anne married Edmund Phelps, a concert singer, and insisted that he should assume the name MacDonnell, which he did by royal consent.

The Devil at Galgorm Castle

There are many strange stories told about the unusual goings-on in and around Galgorm Castle. Sir Faithful Fortescue built the castle near Ballymena in 1618. He was a Jacobite who became quite unpopular with the locals because of his loyalties, and eventually they attacked the castle and

The boot that tricked the devil.

burned down the chapel. Later they sold the land to the Colville family who owned it until the 1800s.

The story most often whispered is that the ghost of Dr Alexander Colville wanders its halls. His appearance is heralded by the sound of footsteps but only made by a single boot. That boot is at the bottom of this tale.

According to the *Ballymena Guardian* newspaper, Dr Colville, while living in Scotland, was a professor of divinity at St Andrew's and in 1622 he was ordained a deacon and priest. In 1636 he became a doctor of divinity and later moved to Ireland, to Coole, where he served his flock for 8 years, from 1626 to 1635, as vicar.

He resigned to take over Skerry and lived in mid-Antrim. In due course he was supposed to buy Galgorm Estate from a Mr Edmond Edmonson and,

since he was considered to be a man of little wealth, the local people were suspicious about his ability to purchase the magnificent castle in 1636. He apparently renamed it Mount Colville.

Rumours abounded about how Dr Colville managed to acquire the large amount of money needed to buy such a residence. Stories of supernatural dealings spread around, particularly amongst those who were jealous of his wealth. One of the strongest rumours was that he was deeply involved in 'black magic' and through this he made contact with the devil. They met by the River Maine, according to legend, and he told the devil he was short of money. In his greed he made a deal with Satan so that he could fulfil his desire to buy and rebuild the castle.

The deal was a rather peculiar one. The devil would go to Colville's house and must give Colville as much gold as could fill a large boot. In return, after 21 years he would leave his earthly life, and at that time the devil would come to claim his soul.

Now Colville was a smart and wily man so he set out to dupe Satan. He cut a hole in the sole of a boot and another in the floor of an upper room. He nailed the boot over the hole in the floor and waited for Satan to come. When he did, Satan kept emptying the gold into the boot not knowing that the gold was filling up the basement of the house. The devil poured the money in, bag after bag, until what he had brought was finally exhausted. He hurried away and it is said that he ordered a legion of demons to sweep the earth and the sea for more treasure with which to fill the boot. After toiling all night he succeeded in filling the boot to the brim. When he had finished, he disappeared, believing that he had the best of the bargain.

No wonder the locals were suspicious of Colville's wealth. They asked themselves how a man of the cloth could possibly acquire so much wealth. The magnificent castle was built and enclosed with a 7-mile wall, which kept Dr Alexander Colville safe until his day of reckoning drew near. But he had few friends in the area, for when word of his dealings with the devil spread, he was shunned. Indeed many inexplicable things happened around the castle and it was said that Colville even introduced some of his servants to the 'black arts'.

But time passed and the day approached when he was to be called upon to repay his debt.

Colville prepared for that day with the same wiliness that he showed when he made the deal with the devil. He lit a candle, sat down on a chair, opened up his Bible and proceeded to read until his co-conspirator appeared to collect his dues. Calmly Colville asked for a last request – to read his Bible until the candle burnt out.

The devil agreed, whereupon Colville put the candle into the Bible and snapped it shut, thus denying the devil his dues, since the candle was safe and the devil is

The Bible and candle that tricked the devil.

not permitted to open the word of God. The candle remained there during the doctor's life and in his will he requested that the Bible should be sealed in a lead box in his coffin on his death.

One supposes that the devil was so ashamed at having been tricked so successfully that he left Galgorm Castle quietly. Whether or not the evil one got his revenge, we will never know but, curiously, when Dr William Young bought Galgorm Castle in 1931, he found a box in the cellar containing a Bible *and* a candle!

So the story of the one-booted footsteps lives on and the ghost of Dr Alexander has apparently not been able to rest in peace in the castle that he coveted during his life. The footsteps sometimes stomp loudly, and at other times visitors have come upon the figure of Colville moving quietly with one boot.

There is a portrait of Colville in the castle, and it is rumoured that if the painting were to leave the castle a strange and terrifying disaster would take place.

The Colville family owned the castle until the 1800s, but after many different owners, it is now a listed historical building and a golf club.

The Banshee of Shane's Castle

There is a sinister message relating to the mysterious black face with a sad expression on the eastern wall of the south-west wing of Shane's Castle. Legend has it that the line of the O'Neill clan will come to an end if the head ever falls from its position on the castle wall. It is thought that this stone carving pre-dates the castle by some centuries. So far the head has not

moved and even though the castle was burnt down in 1816 this tower with the black face survived.

The castle was built in 1345 near Randalstown for the O'Neills of Clanaboy, and its original name of Eden-Dubh-Carraig was changed to Shane's Castle after it was reinstated to the O'Neill clan by King James in 1607. Some sources say that the date of change was much later in 1772.

Neinny Roe, sometimes referred to as Maebhín (Maeveen), the White Lady of Sorrow, is the banshee of the O'Neills and she is said to haunt the castle. Her wailing could be heard heralding the death of every O'Neill right up until the fire. Local tales say that she was the daughter of the chieftain of the O'Neills and traditionally a bedchamber was kept ready for her alone. Apparently this room was allocated to another guest during a large gathering in the castle and Neinny Roe took her revenge by starting a fire in that room to show her displeasure. The flames then spread to the main block of the castle with disastrous consequences.

Another story goes that, as guests were leaving, a Captain Greer, who was the county magistrate, was adamant that he had seen a person dressed in armour pass by the upstairs window. Perhaps Neinny Roe or Maeveen has been blamed in the wrong for the burning. Visitors to the castle bedchamber also nervously reported that they saw the moving indentations of spirits on the bed accompanied by angry noises bouncing from wall to wall inside the room.

Another source suggests that the fairies are to blame for the presence of the banshee (from the Gaelic '*bean-sidhe*', meaning fairy woman). One of the clan

Shane's Castle.

Fairy hawthorn.

The Banshee Maeveen.

keening (from the Gaelic '*ag caoineadh*', meaning 'crying'). Her shriek would be heard upon the shore and along the ruined walls of the castle.

The apparition of Maeveen is said to be quite tall and slender, with blue eyes and blonde hair. This youthful description would strengthen the belief that she was indeed the daughter of the house.

Although the banshee was a young woman and not an old hag, it was still a frightening experience for the person who in 1966 saw a keening and wailing figure bathed in blue-white light.

Maeveen's wailing was also heard in Coile Ultach (the Great Wood of Ulster) through which Shane O'Neill marched his army in 1565 towards the Battle of Glentaisie where he routed the MacDonalds. Historical accounts tell us that many soldiers died en route to the battle and it appears that the lamenting of the wounded and the dying can still be heard in the parts of the woods that remain.

returning to the O'Neill place found a cow struggling to free its horns from a hawthorn tree. Now it is well known that the hawthorn is a sacred tree to the fairies and anything or anyone that becomes entangled in it becomes the property of the fairies. When the clansman cut a branch to release the cow the fairies were extremely upset. This was confirmed when he arrived at his home, for his daughter was gone. Immediately he knew that the fairies had taken her to the Otherworld at the bottom of the nearby Lough Neagh.

The man was so distraught that the fairies bade the girl go back to tell her father that she was safe in the other world and that she would be allowed to return but only to warn of impending death in the family. Since she would not have a human voice she could only do this by

In more recent years many paranormal investigations have been carried out in the tunnels below the castle and in one of them a dark solid form moved quickly through the wall. Thermal cameras have captured images of figures moving on the ramparts in places that are impossible to access. The investigators have been able to record ghostly sounds and one of the most common sensations shared was the cold, clammy and uneasy feeling that someone was standing close by, watching and waiting – for what?

2

DARK HEDGES AND FRIGHTENING PLACES

The Grey Lady of the Dark Hedges

'Tis a fearful thing to be no more,
Or if it be, to wander after death;
To walk as spirits do, in brakes all day;
And when the darkness comes, to glide
in paths
That lead to graves; and, in the silent vault,
Where lies your own pale shroud, to hover o'er it,
Striving to enter your forbidden corpse.

John Dryden, *Oedipus*

Gracehill House.

Avenue of the Dark Hedges.

The beautiful yet strangely mysterious avenue of the beech trees known as the Dark Hedges became famous worldwide when used as one of the locations for the television series *Game of Thrones*.

The Stuart family planted the avenue of over 150 beech trees in the eighteenth century, probably to impress visitors arriving at the mansion known as Gracehill House. James Stuart, who built the dwelling in 1775, named it after his wife Grace Lynd.

The estate on which the house was built has a royal pedigree. King James I granted the land to his cousin James Stuart, who unfortunately died before he could reside there. This beautiful estate then passed to his grandson William Stuart and was the Stuart family home for several years.

The trees provide a welcoming avenue and are a magnificent sight. They tangle and entwine in an amazing arboreal tunnel and in summer the light and shadow in daytime hours are a photographer's dream.

However, at night the tangled gnarled branches that spread from the bent trunks reach across and give one an uneasy sense of the supernatural. It can be an unnerving experience as the eerie branches sway and the path is filled with shadows continually moving. One is inclined to believe that the avenue is truly haunted by the spectre of 'The Grey Lady', for that is how the story goes.

She is said to appear at dusk, hovering between the trees, before gliding to the end of the avenue where she simply fades out of sight. Some speculate that the ghost is a lowly maid who died in strange circumstances, but another legend says that she is a lost spirit from the nearby abandoned graveyard who could not return to her grave on a Halloween night long, long ago.

No one really knows, but few people walk that road at dusk or later for fear of encountering the Grey Lady who wanders between the Dark Hedges.

Nessy O'Haughan, Highwayman and Rebel

Carrickfergus Castle was the place of execution for highwaymen, robbers, traitors and murderers and their demented souls prowl its ramparts and courtyards. It might well be that the headless ghost that haunts the castle is Nessy (Naoise) O'Haughan, who met a fearful death there in 1720 when he was barely 30 years of age.

Nessy was immortalised in a ballad, 'The Bold Outlaw Naoise O'Haughan':

> Tis of a famous highwayman a story
> I will tell,
> His name was Naoise O'Haughan, in
> Ireland he did dwell.
> And on the Antrim Mountains he
> commenced his wild career,
> Where many a wealthy gentleman
> before him shook with fear.

The 1700s were unsafe and uncertain times to live in Ireland. If you did not embrace the Protestant principles of William of Orange whose soldiers roamed the Irish countryside after their victory in the Battle of the Boyne, you were at risk of being killed and your property looted.

Nessy O'Haughan was born in 1691 near Braid at the foot of Slemish Mountain. His father John was a tenant on a hill farm owned by a local landlord. Small farmers were often persecuted and evicted from their homesteads on the flimsiest of excuses. In 1710, bailiffs came to evict the family from the farm for not paying rent due to the landlord and when Nessy and his brothers, Shane Óg, Robert and Denis, and their adopted brother Philomy saw their father being manhandled, they retaliated. In the fracas that followed, Shane Óg killed one of the bailiffs. With that fateful death on their hands they were on the run and became raparees. From that time on Nessy and his brothers were violently antagonistic to any kind of authority.

They sought shelter for their parents among Presbyterian families like the Grahams of Glenwherry, who were sympathetic to their plight. Once they knew that their parents were safe they joined an outlaw band led by Captain McAllister who hailed from Ballynure, not far from their own home place.

But outlaws were zealously hunted and shortly after they joined with McAllister he was captured by troops from Carrickfergus and hanged. Nessy was elected leader of the band of outlaws and they took to the hills. At night they wrecked havoc on the farms and houses of those who toadied to the demands of the landlords and their lackeys.

The outlaws did not simply line their own pockets with the monetary spoils; many acts of generosity and kindness were attributed to them and they often shared money with the poor to help them avoid eviction. They did not ask the religion of those they helped – Presbyterian and Catholic were treated alike – and their loyalty to their friends and neighbours is perhaps the reason that they were able to avoid capture for so long. Those they helped were ever willing to give them shelter.

One story is told about their kindness. Nessy and Shane were out one night in 1718 when they came by a farmer on the road. They held him at sword point but realised that the man was both ill and poor. He told them that he expected to be evicted for not paying his rent. Immediately they gave him the money and although he could not promise to repay them in money he would welcome them into his home.

Even though it was in Glenwherry and Braid that they carried out their 'Robin Hood' activities, their exploits were beginning to torment the rich and powerful in these mid-Antrim valleys. It became obvious to them that paid informers and lackeys were betraying their whereabouts to the authorities and their lives were becoming more and more unsafe. They realised that they were hugely outnumbered and their fellow highwaymen, Toal, Magennis and Rory Murphy, left the country to escape capture. One by one the gang were taken and rewards were paid to the informers. John McCrea of Ballynure, a man they thought of as a friend, received £5 for his part in the capture of Randal Dhu Agnew, a close friend of Nessy's. Randal was hanged at Carrickfergus in 1717.

Nessy O'Haughan refused to bow down to the oppressors and escaped capture many times by sheer daring and bravado. One of his escapes happened near Ballyeaston, when the Redcoats were chasing him. He ducked out of sight of the pursuers, and when he saw a gang of farm workers carrying bags of grain he picked up a bag and walked with them, holding the bag on his shoulder so that he would not be recognised. The Redcoats rode straight by, not realising that they had been outwitted again.

On another occasion, near Knockagh Mountain, he escaped capture when a troop of mounted Redcoats that had been sent from Carrickfergus Castle spied him. Nessy was fleet of foot and he took off, followed by the troop. He ran across the moors at Straid and reached Ballyboley Hill. He was beginning to tire and when he slowed down he came across his brother Denis who was hiding in the heather. Denis, realising that the troop would soon catch Nessy in his exhausted state, whistled to him to swap places.

Nessy rolled into the thick, coarse bracken where Denis covered him and waited. A few moments later the Redcoat troop came into view and Denis took off. The soldiers did not hesitate and chased Denis believing him to be Nessy. Denis, being fresh and just as fleet as his brother, outran the tired mounts of the soldiers ensuring that they both escaped.

Nessy knew, however, that to stay in the same area was too dangerous and he moved to the Divis Mountains. Here he found regular shelter in an area known as Ballyutoag but knowing he could not always depend on good people to keep him in food he raided Craigarogan, Hightown Hill, Ballymagarry, Ballymurphy, Springhill and Ballyhill. He managed to elude his pursuers many more times and found shelter in the caves of Black Mountain below Hatchet Field.

Little did he know it then but his prowess at running and jumping would be his future undoing. He was chased across the Belfast Hills right to the edge of the Six Mile Water, a wide and rough stream that was too wide to jump and too turbulent to swim across. The jubilant officer thought that he had finally cornered Nessy but at the last moment

Nessy O' Haughan's hideout.

Nessy backed up a few feet and took a wide wild leap, managing to land on the other side. The water was too wide even for the horses to jump and his pursuers turned disconsolately away, foiled once again.

Apparently Nessy was tired of being hunted and enlisted in the army of King George under an alias. One day when the regiment was stationed at Louth, field sports were being held. Nessy's company was unfortunately beaten in the jumping contest and the captain was very annoyed. He asked if any one would volunteer to restore the pride of the company. Without thinking, Nessy stepped forward and took up the challenge whereupon he jumped clear over three horses, breaking the record and upholding the honour of his company. A dragoon who had been in the party that chased Nessy to the Six Mile Water shouted out, 'No one could have done that but Nessy O'Haughan.'

The soldiers gathered round and Nessy was arrested, taken to Carrickfergus, tried and convicted. The judge sentenced him to be hanged with six of his former confederates on the Gallows Green in 1720. As a warning to others their heads were

The Ballyboley Forest Apparitions

The raven and the skull.

Outside Larne there is a haunted forest called Ballyboley. According to legend it was once an important site for Druid worship. The distinctive marks of this are stone formations and circular trenches, which are still obvious even though the forest floor is well grown over. As for the pagan worship of the Druids, some might well argue that it was not far from demonic practice – bizarre sacrifices, kidnappings, perhaps even murders.

It appears that from the 1400s to the 1700s as many as thirty people in the locality vanished after entering the forest and no one has ever been able to provide an explanation for these frightening and weird disappearances. Some believe that there is a doorway to the Celtic 'otherworld' within the forest, and to leave one of the well-trodden paths is to court the wrath of the malevolent spirits who reside there.

During its history there have been frightening reports of strange shadowy figures, both human and animal, lurking in the trees, watching, waiting and stalking the unwary travellers who enter the forest. Many people have said that they find themselves overcome by unease and dread that they cannot explain – a sensation of being watched, even though they cannot see anyone.

Ballyboley Forest's eerie history of apparitions and disappearances is one that cannot be ignored. In 1994 one couple heard the sound of screaming voices quite close to them and fled in fear when a mass of shadowy cloud appeared in front of them without warning.

In 1997 a newspaper reported that two ramblers walking in the forest heard

cut off and spiked upon the courthouse.

Some say that his brother Shane O'Haughan was betrayed by his brother-in-law 'White' James McKinstry for £10 and suffered the same punishment at Gallows Green, Carrickfergus. It is said too that a wren built its nest in Shane's skull and that a raven picked out his eyes.

Many years after the execution, when the building was being used as a school and there was a classroom beneath the gable where the outlaws' heads had been spiked, and one stormy night, Nessy's head rolled down the chimney, terrifying the children the next day.

Other tales tell of a headless man circling the old well in the castle, a castle known to be one of the most haunted in Ireland.

a very loud flapping noise that continually followed them. At first they just accepted it as normal forest sounds but other noises intruded and made them stop. They distinctly heard a woman moaning as if in great pain and left the path to investigate. The cries and moans became more distressed and when they entered the small clearing from which the sounds seemed to have been coming the noise stopped abruptly and there was total silence, no birds, no animals and no person to be seen. Puzzled, they looked around and the most unnerving ear-splitting scream shook the air.

At the same moment they saw that the nearby trees were heavily smeared and dripping with blood. Terrified, they took to their heels but when another scream rent the air one of the ramblers looked behind him and to his horror saw four figures standing motionless where there had been none only seconds before. They were clothed in dark, ragged cassock-type clothes and their heads were bowed

and covered. Although the man could not see their faces he said that he knew they were definitely staring at him.

But it was not only adults who heard strange noises and saw weird figures. A woman reported that she and a group of young people camped in the forest as part of an award scheme in 2005. When dusk was falling, some of them mentioned that they saw some people moving between the trees about a five-minute walk away and when they went to investigate there was nothing. Sometime later, as they sat around the campfire, they noticed four figures again in the same place, but this time they were carrying torches that looked like tree branches set on fire rather than mechanical ones. The figures then disappeared into the trees and they heard sounds in the distance, like the cries and squeals of animals one might have heard during an ancient slaughtering ritual.

In the morning light they dismissed these experiences, but later, when the

The eerie figures of Ballyboley Forest.

woman read a report in a newspaper featured on a website called *The Shadowlands*, she knew they had witnessed a ghostly apparition and every hair on her body stood on end.

The Grey Man's Path

The north coast is steeped in myths, legends and tales of the supernatural and Fair Head, one of the most majestic headlands in Ireland, is one such area. A well-known landmark is the Grey Man's Path (or Casan an Fhir Leith) and a peculiar story is told about this treacherous fissure on the face of Benmore. The path runs from above Fair Head, passes beyond Loch Dhu (the Dark Lake) down through the ravine locally known as the Grey Man's Gulley, right down to the shore.

The entrance to the path at the top is very narrow and became known as Mary McAnulty's Hall Door. This was a reference to an old lady who gathered dulse, a type of edible seaweed, from the shore. She used the path daily and was able to eke out a living selling the dried dulse in the market of Ballycastle. (Dulse is still one of the popular delicacies sold at the Auld Lammas Fair in Ballycastle.)

One of the stories regarding this area tells us that Mary had an encounter with a strange man one evening as darkness began to fall. Although she knew the path well and even on a gloomy evening was as sure-footed as a sheep, she felt a strange unease and stopped to take a rest at one of her regular resting places. The full bag of seaweed seemed heavier than usual and as she lowered it to the ground she noticed a figure approach in her direction along the path.

The Grey Man's Path. *(Etching,* Dublin Penny Journal)

Immediately she lifted the bag and slinging it over her shoulder she walked cautiously, knowing that she would have to pass him on the narrow path. She noticed that he was limping and that his face was very pale and set. He did not look at her, nor smile or return her greeting, but hid his face further beneath the hood of his cloak.

Mary hurried on, as fast as her load would allow, planning to stop at Loch Dhu to rest. A mist had begun to creep in from the sea and she shivered. She would have stumbled had not a hand at her elbow steadied her. She looked around. The stranger had silently caught up with her and as she turned to thank him he averted his face. He brushed her thanks aside and asked where she was going.

'Home,' she answered, 'but I need to rest first.'

He remained with her and when she sat at her usual place at Loch Dhu, he sat down beside her with a weary sigh. She tried not to stare but in the fading light she glimpsed his face and it was grey.

'Are you ill?' she asked but he only gazed across the waters of the loch and did not answer. His hood loosened and she saw that his hair had an unusual greenish tinge. Without thinking she asked him the reason and he answered very simply in a voice that was like none she had ever heard before. He pointed to Loch Dhu and said that he had lived beneath the waters there and that was the reason for his strange appearance.

Mary didn't believe him and thought that he must have had too much to drink or perhaps was somewhat deranged, so she rose again to walk home but the man accompanied her. He did not speak again. When she sat down once more to rest, he sat beside her saying that he was very tired. He lay against her bag of dulse and put his head on her lap and to her astonishment he fell asleep.

In the gathering darkness she began to fear that this stranger could do her harm. She looked around but there was no one in sight. She tried to ease her body away but he stirred and then she noticed that his leg was twisted strangely. On closer inspection she was horrified to notice that his foot was actually a cloven hoof that was mangled and broken. She felt the fear rise in her and terrified that he might wake she inched his head from her lap and managed to slip her leg out from under it. His skin felt coarse and slimy to the touch but she persevered and in a few moments she had disentangled herself and ran off, her breath coming in gasps and her heart pounding with the fear of feeling his hand on her arm as she had before.

When she arrived at her cottage she thrust her hands into a bucket of cleansing water and locked the door, praying that God would deliver her from the grey devil that slept on the path to the shore. At that moment an awful spine-chilling scream echoed across the headland and the wind and rain lashed at her window and the storm battered at her door. Only when dawn broke did it settle and Mary ventured outside. On the grass were hoof prints as if a horse had trampled there in a frenzy.

Mary never ventured down the path in the evening again after her encounter with the grey devil, nor did she pass Loch Dhu without thinking of her escape.

It is said that the spectre of the Grey Man is seen when the mist rolls in from the sea and he takes on a human form to wander along Murlough Bay and Grey Man's Gully waiting to lure some unsuspecting passer-by into the otherworld that lies beneath the dark waters of Loch Dhu.

There is another account given of the Grey Man appearing near the mouth of the Bush River. Two youths were fishing for trout late one evening when a man appeared quite suddenly nearby. They hadn't seen or heard him approach but he seemed harmless enough and they continued casting out their lines.

One of the young men was about to make conversation when he noticed that the man's body cast no reflection on the water. He whispered to his companion to look and his companion saw that this was true. They hurriedly began to pack up their gear. The man looked at them with piercing, staring eyes and, petrified with fear, they found themselves unable to move.

The man waded into the shallows and only then did they see what they believed to be a cloven foot. This was not an ordinary man. Still hypnotised by his gaze, they were unable to tear their eyes away until their dog jumped and barked.

They ran off and never returned there to fish.

The Phantom Coach of Dundermot Mound

What would entice a man to bring his young daughter on an 80-mile journey by coach from Belfast to Derry? Whatever it was it must have been extremely important and he was handsomely paid for the errand.

The rebellion by the United Irishmen around 1799 was well underway, but some Belfast merchants who had been staunch supporters of the movement began to worry about the economic consequences of such a rebellion and abandoned the cause. It appears that they wished to let the army garrisoned in Derry know so that there would be no retribution against them. To that end, they hired Thomas McHarg to deliver a parcel and letter to the Derry barracks.

As the coach made its way through the country on a January night, light snowfall turned into a blizzard. The driver decided to stop at an inn in Antrim to change horses rather than travelling on to Moore's Inn in Ballymena. The innkeeper and his wife asked McHarg to stay for the night in the hope that the storm would pass before morning, but he refused, even though the innkeeper's wife begged him to think of his daughter.

'The poor wee girl is nearly dead with cold. Won't you stay, have a hot supper and set off in the morning?'

Dundermot Mound and the phantom coach.

But Thomas McHarg was not to be persuaded. He was promised a generous bonus if he delivered the package within two days and he was not about to let anything stop him. So, he wrapped his daughter in a blanket, closed the door of the coach, hitched up a fresh team of horses and swung himself up into the driver's seat.

The innkeeper made a last plea for him to stay but he insisted on journeying onwards with the words 'Neither God nor the devil himself can keep me from getting to Derry'.

The weather got worse but McHarg pushed on until he approached a village near the Clough River. It was his intention to cross at Glarryford where there was a small inn but the snow had turned to rain and he knew there was a possibility the bridge might be damaged. With this in mind he stopped the coach at Cullybacky and asked two other travellers, 'Is the Glarryford Bridge down?'

One answered that it was but the other man wasn't sure and suggested that he should take a detour to the other bridge near Dundermot Mound. Thomas was reluctant to do so because the bridge there was narrower and it also had a very sinister reputation. He whipped up the horses and after another few miles he stopped another traveller and asked the same question, 'Is the Glarryford Bridge down?' The man didn't know.

Reluctantly, McHarg took the detour to the other bridge but inexplicably he, his daughter and the coach and horses were never seen again. Legend has it that as he passed the mound he was swallowed or dragged into a secret entrance to hell it and was lost forever.

The Dundermot Mound was apparently the site of many demonic rituals and sacrifices and it is thought that on certain nights of the year the entrance to the world of darkness and terror opens up, releasing all sorts of beasts onto the earth.

It is also said that the entrance opens to allow Black Tom's coach to return to entice other travellers into the other world. If you should encounter the coach along the road and hear the driver ask, 'Is the Glarryford Bridge down?', do not answer, for if you do, or speak one word to him, it is said you will die within a year. Worse still, this phantom could drag you into the dark recesses of the world of demons.

The Cursed Fort

The ruins of the old fort of Dun-a-Mallaght are in the grounds of the Boyd family's ancestral home, Manor House, on the eastern slope of Glentow, a few miles from Ballycastle. The fort or rath is a flat-topped mound known as the Cursed Fort or the Fairy Fort.

There is a story behind both of these names. It all began in the ballroom of Roger O'Carroll's tavern in Ann Street, Ballycastle on an Easter Tuesday in the early 1800s. There was a ceilidh following the fair day and everyone was enjoying the singing and dancing until early morning.

After the dancing a group of four girls and two men sat down to rest and the chat soon turned to stories they had heard from the old folk. One of the men said that he had no belief in fairies at all and the girls argued that there were many places about known to be fairy raths.

'Well,' said Daniel McCurdy, 'I go to those places you mentioned to catch

Present day Céilidhe dancing.

hares and rabbits and I've never noticed the slightest trace of any fairies about there. You're listening to too many old wives' tales.'

One of the girls insisted that fairies were seen and heard at the old fort of Dun-a-Mallaght, especially on May Eve.

The discussion went on and eventually the four girls arranged that they would go to the fort at midnight on May Eve and dance blindfolded for an hour. After some persuasion the two men agreed to accompany them. The plan was that they would go as far as the banks of the Tow stream, put bandages over the girls' eyes and when that was done the men would lead them across the bridge and leave them a short distance from the fort. After that the men would move back to a place where they had a clear view of the fort. The girls were excited because they had persuaded Daniel, the doubter, to buy them each a silver watch if the fairies made an appearance. Daniel

agreed, confident in the belief that nothing would happen.

When the six of them set off around ten o'clock at night on May Eve the sky was clear and the moon was bright enough to light their way. Having arrived, the girls were blindfolded and led to the rath and the men retired as planned. All the while they could hear the girls giggling and laughing and occasionally chanting, 'This is the home of the fairies; this is the home of the fairies.'

The men smiled and were remarking to each other about the silliness of the girls when suddenly a strange disturbance filled the air, like the sound of hundreds of flapping wings. A pale, luminous yellow light floated towards them from the glen. When it passed overhead they were astonished to see dozens of little figures with human features. Indeed, it was so unexpected and inexplicable that the men were dumbfounded and struck silent. One little figure stood on top of the old fort and others danced around in a curious rhythm accompanied by hypnotic low music.

The two men, not hearing the girls's voices, began to fear for their safety. They made several attempts to reach the fort but on each occasion a dense darkness enveloped them and they were unable to move forward. On the fourth attempt a weird sound rose from the fort and they fell down into a trance.

When they awoke the next morning each was lying in his own bed. Daniel rushed to his friend's house and they were both puzzled and anxious when they also discovered that none of the four girls had returned home. Straight away they set off in search of them and came upon three of the girls lying in the centre of the fort. Their hair was strewn everywhere and it seems they were asleep and clasping hands.

Daniel approached and, fearful that they might not be alive, he gently touched their foreheads with his finger, at which they opened their eyes and rose to their feet, all the while gazing upwards to the sky.

Only when the men led them gently across the bridge did they emerge from their trance-like state and ask where their fourth companion was. The men told them what had happened the previous night and that their friend was still missing.

Naturally the girls were distressed at the news and when pressed told the men what they had experienced. They explained that as soon as the fairies arrived over the fort they felt sleep creeping over them. When they lay down they held hands and sweet melodious music filled their senses. After a short time two of the girls felt the hands of the youngest being unclasped and her hair being untangled from theirs. They had no other recollection of the night but from that fateful May Eve the young girl was never again seen.

However, it is said that every May Eve at midnight six knocks sound on the door of the house where she lived in Milltown near Ballycastle and the form of a young girl dressed in white flowing garments walks six times in front of the

house floating a little above the ground. She does not seem unhappy; rather she sings the same music that the girls heard on the night she was abducted. Later that century the poet William Allingham wrote his famous fairy poem based on a similar story:

Up the airy mountain,
Down the rushy glen,
We dare not go a-hunting
For fear of little men;
Wee folk and good folk
Trooping all together.
Green jacket, red cap,
And white owl's feather.

Nowadays not many would dare risk walking near Cursed Fort on May Eve and no one has ever discovered the young girl's fate.

Haunted Long Lane, Belfast

Long Lane is now gone but in the 1800s it was the main route to Carrickfergus. It was an entry running from North Street, in Belfast, to Church Street and, even though it was a laneway just wide enough to accommodate the coach and horses that used it, it was a very busy thoroughfare. Daily, men and women from the outskirts of Belfast pushed their carts along the lane to the markets.

Pickpockets and beggars frequented the street especially in the late evening when the market traders passed on their way homewards. It was a poor area but there were at least three other businesses on the lane, and the cotton mill owned by Robert Gemmill employed many workers who came to Belfast from the rural areas. They often worked late into the night but most were wary of walking the lane alone after dark.

Sometimes after a good day of trading in the market, men would stop at William Skelton's tavern at No. 2 Long Lane. Unfortunately many men drank the day's takings instead of going straight home. But this was not the case with Fred Orr. He was a hard worker and provided as best he could for his wife and children. Even in the cold days of winter he filled his cart with whatever produce he had, harnessed his donkey to it and made his way to the market in Belfast where he stayed until everything was sold.

One dark winter's evening his mind was on his wife's welcome and the supper and warm fire waiting for him in his cottage. He did not see the two men waiting in the shadow of the doorway of Robert Millican's saddlers. As he passed, they stole out of hiding, pounced on him and beat him to the ground with heavy wooden weapons. Bleeding and semi-conscious, he could not stop them from stealing the money he had made at the market.

Before they fled into the night they chased the donkey away and left Fred lying wounded on the cobbled street. He pulled himself to his feet and staggered a few yards calling out for help but he sank to the ground as the sleet turned to snow. Some of the women who had worked late at the mill passed by thinking that Fred was just another man who had drunk himself into a stupor in the tavern.

It was not until the next morning when they returned to work that they found poor Fred's frozen body, which caused the more caring amongst them some angst.

Molly, his wife, came searching for him when the donkey returned home

A murderer's self-imposed punishment.

on its own. When she discovered the fate of her dear husband she cursed the people who had done the terrible deed and called on her dead husband to wreak vengeance on them.

Some months later, as summer approached, a man was found dead in Long Lane, and although there was no sign of any wounds on his person, the grotesque expression on his face told of something horribly frightening and terrible enough to cause his death.

Words were whispered that he was one of the men who had killed Fred Orr. He was well known in the area as a drunken ruffian not above stealing and bullying, but few would speak out against him when he was alive for fear of reprisals.

'Good riddance,' was the general comment at the time. The stories began to circulate that Orr's ghost was returning to seek revenge on his killers and indeed strange things began to happen to the other man. In his hovel of a house he often heard and felt the presence of someone, but when he called out no one answered. On another occasion the bucket of water that he'd fetched from the pump was red when he reached home. Worst of all was his vision of a ghostly figure with a bloodied head, staggering about Long Lane when he ventured out.

He was not the only person to see the ghostly figure. Some of the women from the mill saw him in the gloom of the evening. He was begging for help and disappeared before they reached him.

A year to the day after the terrible crime, the second man who had taken part passed the spot where they had murdered Fred Orr. According to two women workers who were on their way home he turned a ghastly shade of grey and began to scream. He ran away as if the devil was at his heels.

His body was found the next day, dangling from a beam in a yard as the rats ran around below, screeching.

It is said that with this man's suicide the ghostly appearances ceased in Long Lane. Still, even though the area has changed … in the dark winter evenings, it can still be an eerie and disturbing place.

3

ILL-FATED LOVERS

The Tragic Lovers of Giant's Causeway

> The ghosts … are calling to each other
> thro' a dawn
> Stranger than earth has ever seen; the
> veil
> Is rending, and the Voices of the day
> Are heard across the Voices of the dark.
>> Alfred Lord Tennyson, 'The Ring'

Most famous places have their tragedies and Giant's Causeway is no exception. In the 1880s, a guidebook about the Causeway told the story of the ghost of a poor young woman who fell to her death from the high cliff above the causeway.

The poor girl, by the name of Peggy, was betrothed to William, a young fisherman. The sea around the north coast is particularly treacherous, but William was

Giant's Causeway.

anxious to earn money for their future life together. So, he went to sea in all weathers but he was known to be steady and trustworthy and could be depended upon to keep a cool head in a storm.

Peggy did not shirk from the hard work that would bring their life together nearer. She spent her days gathering kelp from the sea where it grew in underwater 'forests' along the rocky coast of North Antrim.

For many people in the area gathering kelp was their only livelihood and after a north-east gale it was particularly plentiful at the shallow stretch of the coast near the Giant's Causeway.

It was hard work for the men who cut it from the rocks with long-handled knives. Using drag hooks with shafts 20 foot in length and with three prongs they dragged it to the shore. Once the kelp was above the water level, women and children began pulling it ashore where they spread it out to dry.

During a week or two of good weather the kelp would be shaken and turned to completely dry out, after which it would be ready to be moved. Women bound the dried bundles and carried the loads on their heads up the almost perpendicular path to the cliff top.

On a still day the smoke from hundreds of kelp fires climbed into the sky in columns that resembled the basalt columns below on the Causeway. When it was burnt the kelp left an ash of much valued sodium carbonate, which farmers spread on their fields to neutralise acidic soil.

It was a terribly dangerous way to earn money and the women prayed for dry weather for there was less chance of losing one's footing on the perilous pathway when it was dry. The climb

A kelp gatherer on the Causeway coast.

upwards must have been very difficult and backbreaking – one guide compared the line of women toiling upwards to 'mice crawling up the wall of a barn'.

Peggy was fair and delicate but was determined to work as long as she had the strength to do so. However, one damp day when the kelp weighed heavier than usual she set off along the path balancing it on her head. A woman behind her noticed that the bundle had begun to loosen and saw Peggy struggling to hold it steady. The poor girl paused just as she got to the steepest spot and the woman said her strength seemed to fail her and she sank down.

She tried to remove the load of kelp from Peggy's back but in its loosened state it fell and Peggy, in trying to save it, toppled over. The woman behind her,

The white mist on the cliffs.

burdened by her own load, watched helplessly as the heavy weight caused Peggy to fall awkwardly and her body bounced off the rocky cliff like a rag doll.

As she lay at the bottom, bloody and broken from her fall, other women who were lining up to ascend the cliff path ran to her but there was nothing they could do. Peggy was beyond help.

At sea, William had an awful premonition that something terrible had happened and he rowed as fast as he could to the shore. When he beached the boat he rushed towards the people gathered in a group. Some of the men tried to shield him from the sight of his beloved's body but he pushed his way through only to find that his fears were well founded. He knelt beside her and she took her last breath whispering the name of her betrothed.

Peggy was laid to rest in the dress she had made for her wedding and her friends, the kelp gatherers, attended her funeral. Naturally, William was inconsolable and soon afterwards, odd to relate, the young man's boat capsized and he joined his beloved Peggy in death.

It is said that on a clear still night his heartbroken cry is heard echoing along the Cliff Walk at Giant's Causeway and that sometimes from the rocks where Peggy fell, a white mist whirls to the top of the cliff as if the sky itself is weeping.

The Legends of Dunluce Castle

> 'The banshee was supposed to have been an ancestor of the person whose death she deigned to forewarn.'
> O'Kearney, *The Battle of Gabhra*, 1855

A long time ago, during the fifteenth century to be exact, a tale unfolded in

Dunluce Castle. It is a story of passion and tells of the tragedy of two young people who fell in love. It is a tale of lives destroyed by a father's pride. It is a tale to rival *Romeo and Juliet*.

Richard Óg de Burgo, 2nd Earl of Ulster, built this majestic castle in the thirteenth century on the dramatic and commanding cliffs of the north Antrim coast about midway between Portrush and Giant's Causeway. This iconic ruin perched on the cliff top has witnessed many battles and sieges in its tumultuous history. Wild waves thunder through the sheer deep chasm that almost separates it from the mainland and in the rocks far below the castle, close to the sea, lies the Mermaid's Cave.

The castle is a forbidding sight even on a summer's day. In the fifteenth century, McQuillan, the Lord of Dunluce, had a daughter called Maeve. Her mother died when she was barely 10 years old, but Maeve had inherited her compassion and love for the poor. She was known throughout the estate to be gentle and charitable. From the age of 15, she rose at dawn and spent her time helping the destitute poor, particularly those who lived on the estate.

One day, burdened by a heavy basket, she met a handsome young man. He offered to carry her basket and accompanied her around the estate. Each morning thereafter, she met him and very soon the young couple were deeply in love.

There was an air of mystery about him and although Maeve was quite open about who she was, he told her only that his name was Reginald. Where he came from she did not know, but when McQuillan heard of the meetings he forbade her to see the young man. She cried bitterly and when her father informed her that he had plans to wed her to the son of a rich and powerful neighbour she was almost prostrate with grief.

Maeve swore to her father that she would rather die than marry someone she did not love. Her father, terrified that she would elope with this mysterious young man, decided to lock her up in

The stark ruins of Dunluce Castle.

The Mermaid's Cave.

one of the castle's towers. There, all she could do to fill her days was to sweep her room and make her bed. Her food was passed through a grille in the door and all of the servants except one were forbidden to speak with her.

She begged this servant to bring wool to her and began to knit a long white gown. One day her father found her at work on it and asked her if it was her bridal gown.

She replied, 'No, Father, it is my shroud.'

Her father was beside himself with rage at what he considered her impertinence.

'Stay here then,' he shouted, 'and sweep your room until you see sense!'

As time passed the servants reported to her father that she was wasting away. He was greatly concerned and came to the door. She refused to open it.

'If you say that you will wed the noble man I have chosen for you, I promise that you shall have your freedom.'

No sound except the scratching of a broom on the floor came from her room. He knocked loudly on the door again.

'What is your decision?' he asked.

'If I cannot marry the man I love, I will remain here and sweep my room.'

'You are wasting my time and yours. How long can you remain there?'

'Forever.'

'And your shroud?'

'When it is finished, you shall see me dressed in it.'

McQuillan realised that her will was stronger than his but his pride would not let him accede to her wishes. Daily he grew more remorseful as the servants' stories of her decline reached his ears. If he did not give in she would lose her life. He sent envoys to find out who the mysterious young man was. When they reported that he was a person of some standing, being of noble birth and a member of the rich O'Cahan clan, McQuillan deliberated on how he could save his child and keep his pride. So, he devised a plan.

One morning he left the castle with a contingent of soldiers, telling his servants that he would not return for some days. Soon afterwards, Maeve heard the key turning in the lock. Angry at being caught weeping, she turned on the servant. He put his finger to his lips to silence her and beckoned her to follow him.

'Your young man is waiting,' said the servant.

He led her to the Mermaid's Cave below the fort where Reginald greeted her and paid the servant who had freed her. As he helped his beloved Maeve into the small boat he was shocked at her emaciated body. He realised that he had come to rescue her just in time and cursed her father for doing such a cruel injustice to his daughter. Full of righteous anger he pushed off from the rock where the boat had been waiting.

As if the weather understood young Reginald's dark mood it began to change. Wind roared across the stormy sea and thunder and lightening split the air.

Maeve tried to help Reginald pull the oars but their boat was small and she was too frail. The little craft rose and dipped as the sea swirled around it. Against a ferocious wind and enormous waves, Reginald did his utmost to keep the craft afloat.

The servant who had freed the girl had been McQuillan's accomplice in his master's plan to restore life and happiness to his daughter, without in any way sacrificing his pride. McQuillan rejoiced to have concocted this plan of pretending to leave, but secretly re-entering the castle.

As he reached her room and crossed to the window to watch her escape he became very afraid at the scene that was unfolding. He kept his eyes on the tiny boat being buffeted by the raging sea and he uttered a prayer.

'Lord, I have driven my daughter from her home because of my pride. They only think of their love and not of their future, but at least, dear Lord, I have saved her from a wasting death.'

At that moment McQuillan saw the boat being tossed from the top of an angry wave into the surging trough below. Horrified and paralysed with fear, he searched the sea with his eyes but the boat had disappeared. He called out to his men to launch their long boat to save her but it was too late. She had disappeared forever beneath the merciless sea.

In the weeks following that dreadful day, McQuillan, out of his mind with grief, walked along the shore calling his daughter's name, but only the wind answered him.

One day as he walked with a bowed head along the beach searching for some sign that his daughter was still alive, a strange thought or premonition made him look up to the castle. He stopped, astounded.

His sad-eyed daughter Maeve was at the bars of the window of the tower where she had shed so many tears. She was dressed in her shroud and held her broom in her hand. The ghostly figure showed him her shroud, saying, 'It is finished, as you see.'

Pitifully, her father cried, 'For how long will you stay?'

'Forever' came her reply, and thus she became the banshee of the McQuillan family.

A small boat in an angry sea.

In his book, *The Three Kingdoms: England, Scotland, Ireland*, published in 1844, Charles Victor P. Arlincourt wrote:

> Beneath the immense fortress is a cavern of proportionate vastness; its vault is more than sixty feet high, and its length exceeds three hundred feet. The sea enters it with a roaring sound. Above is the dread tower, where the Banshee of the McQuillans, the ancient lords of Dunluce, appears. I passed under its walls; there is the turret of Maeva. I was desired to remark how carefully it was swept. 'Who undertakes that office?' I asked. 'No living being,' was the answer. 'Every night this prison-like chamber is cleaned like a ball-room, and yet no one enters it.' 'Who then keeps it in order?' 'Meava, the sweeper of Dunluce, and the Banshee of the McQuillans.

Afterwards the castle passed onto Sorley Boy MacDonnell after the Battle of Orla in 1565, but almost 20 years later, in 1584, Queen Elizabeth I commanded Sir John Perrot to retake Dunluce. He did so but caused terrible damage by bombarding the castle with cannon fire. When Sorley Boy was finally evicted, Perrot installed Peter Carey as the caretaker constable much to the disgust of the queen. Within a year, Queen Elizabeth reinstated Sorley Boy MacDonnell in the castle. His first act was to hang Carey from the South East Tower for all to mock the much-hated constable.

Legend has it that the ghost of Peter Carey clad in a purple cloak wanders the tower, bemoaning his ignominious fate.

In 1635 Sorley Boy's grandson Randall brought his wife Catherine Manners to the castle, but from the first time that she cast eyes on its dark fortified walls she hated it. As the wife of the late Duke of Buckingham, she enjoyed court life in London, and the castle, with the ever-present sound of waves pounding below, was overwhelming. The fact that she was Countess of Antrim and wife of the 2nd Earl did not make up for the social life she led in London.

In 1639, while they were residing in Dunluce, part of the castle including the kitchens fell into the sea; several cooks and servants died a horrible death as they plummeted onto the rocks. One man, an itinerant cobbler, was said to have survived by cowering in a corner of the vanished room. He reported that the wild wailing of the banshee filled the kitchens before they crumbled and he was bodily picked up and flung into a corner by the banshee who had the beautiful face of a young girl.

Thereafter the Countess of Antrim refused to live in Dunluce again. In 1690 after the Battle of the Boyne, which led to the impoverishment of the McDonnell who had adhered to the cause of James II, Dunluce Castle was abandoned and the wind, rain and waves gradually reduced it to the lonely ruin that it is today.

But they say that one can still hear Maeve's broom sweeping in the ruins on a quiet, calm day and on stormy nights when the wind wails and the waves crash onto the rocks her heartbroken cries can be heard.

Visitors also speak of the cold chill of an unseen presence in the South-East Tower. But strange things continue to happen in the castle shop – members of staff have found that books have been lifted and rearranged, sometimes on the shelves and sometimes on the floor and radios have mysteriously switched on during the night to play a sad lament.

The Ghost of Young Helena Blunden

During the nineteenth century, many people flocked into Belfast to work in the mills to escape the uncertainty of the agricultural life. Textile mills were harsh places and linen mills were probably amongst the worst in which to work. By 1890 more than 50,000 people worked in the linen industry.

Although Helena Blunden's family moved to England shortly after her birth, her father was drawn back to Ireland in 1911 to a small house in Raphael Street. This was a small street in the Markets Area of Belfast, just a few hundred yards from a linen mill.

Like most girls, Helena, at the age of 16, began to work in the spinning room of the mill. It was a tough life for a young girl. The rooms were wet and

The banshee of the McQuillan's.

The Haunted Mill.

the facilities were awful. The workers were only allowed to use the lavatory, called 'the wee house', in the direst of circumstances and only after they had tied up all the thread ends on the looms. The air was stale and condensation settled on the walls and floors making them treacherous. The workers usually went bare-footed rather than destroy their shoes since most were poor and unable to afford the luxury of decent clothes or shoes.

Helena rarely complained about the arduous and repetitive work of the spinning room, even though the temperature in the hot summers almost reached boiling point and many women and children fainted from heatstroke. She was a popular and hard-working girl and sang against the loud noise of the machinery. When other women were at breaking point Helena was always there with a word of encouragement and a song to brighten their day.

Helena worked a 60-hour week, with only one short break for lunch each day, and although the workers were supposed to finish work on Saturday at twelve o'clock they were made to stay late and even work on Sundays if an important order needed to be completed.

She had aspirations to be an entertainer on the stage one day and was encouraged by her father although her mother frowned upon that. Still, she learnt off the poetry of W. B. Yeats and practised her acting at home in the plays of Bernard Shaw. She often entertained her fellow workers with the bawdy songs of the English music halls, behind the foremen's backs, of course.

On Sunday, 14 April 1912, Helena's exuberance was clear to all.

'I'm going to a concert in the Grand Opera House,' she sang out and threw herself into the work of helping to finish a special order for Argentina. But things did not go to plan: the machine jammed and by the time the spinners were able to continue with the order Helena knew that her work would not be finished by six o'clock. There would be very little time between finishing her work and going to the Opera House. In an attempt to save time Helena kept her shoes on as she worked, hoping to dash out as soon as the work was completed.

The spinners and weavers worked in the rooms at the machines but another woman called Margaret Maxwell was employed to mop and clean condensation off the walls and stairs. She was not a pleasant person, used to fighting and brawling in the streets after working in the flax house, and she resented being unfit for that work any longer. She saw the cleaning work as demeaning and complained fiercely if anyone walked on the stairs while she cleaned. Most of the women ignored her threats and insults and advised Helena to do the same, even though Margaret Maxwell was particularly insolent to her, deriding her English accent and her singing voice.

On that Sunday a young half-timer began to walk down the stairs as the cleaner half-heartedly sluiced the mop to and fro. Margaret screamed at her and marched off in rage, leaving the mop lying there.

At seven o'clock on the dot, Helena joyfully bounded towards the stairs. In her excitement she did not see the abandoned mop. She tripped and tumbled

The Grand Opera House, Belfast.

down to the ground floor, screaming as she fell. Margaret Maxwell, sulking two floors below, watched her fall. She rushed to the bottom of the stairs where Helena's body lay broken and still. Margaret Maxwell never forgave herself for causing the young girl's fatal accident.

Helena Blunden's fellow workers were devastated by her death, knowing that they would never now see their rising star on stage. They missed her sweet voice, which had made the noise and misery of the mill bearable, but it is said that soon after her death they heard her singing and felt her presence.

Although the flax house is no longer a mill but a printing company, many people say that her voice can still be faintly heard singing on the stairs and in the room that was once the spinning room. Her ghost has been sighted several times on a web camera, which was placed in the building by a paranormal group and was recording constantly for over a year.

One of the employees has apparently heard thumps and doors opening and closing and footsteps on the bare wooden floors even though no one else was in the building. Mr McAvoy, who works in the flax house, was operating the press and felt someone tapping his shoulder. He turned around, but the room was empty. He also said that he heard a woman's voice call his name in the basement, but when he and his colleagues checked the room it was empty.

The last person out of the print works each evening had, we believe, the task of turning off all the lights and the radio but regularly, when the door was opened in the morning, the lights were blazing and the radio blaring. There was no explanation for that other than it being the work of the ghost believed to be that of the young girl Helena Blunden.

A few years ago a linen bundle was found on the premises containing a 100-year-old recording of Helena singing 'Pie Jesu' and a newspaper review reporting that the recording was made in 1912, just 3 months before her untimely death.

The Lord of Dunluce

The Lord of Dunluce to the hunting is gone,
The hare and the wild deer his quarry;
He hunted o'er brake, o'er moorland and lawn
Till he came to the loughs of Carey.

In Ireland's wide zone there is no spot so lone,
On Antrim's dark hill none so dreary,
The east winds there moan o'er the moss-covered stone,
The sound of the tempest is eerie.

Down from his horse sprang the Lord of Dunluce,
And down sprang his huntsmen so merry,
With 'Here we will stay till the sun's latest ray
Disappears o'er the far hills o' Derry.'

Then up and out spake an old huntsman: 'I pray,
Dear Master of mine, be you weary,
And do not thou stay till the dawn of the day
By the fearsome dark loughs of Carey.

'For out of the lough comes a spirit of guile,
In the guise of a fair young maiden,
With a languishing glance and a roseate smile,
Her lithe limbs gay garments arrayed in.

And woe to the bouchal this maiden admires,
If he for a season should tarry
His heart is consumed by Love's fierce inward fires,
He wanders distraught over Carey.'

'Tis an old wife's tale,' said the Lord of Dunluce;
'Little I heed it and less I fear;
I would build me a hut if the winds make truce,
And a spirit would never come near.

'So build me a bothy of the hazel boughs,
And cover it over with heather,

And there I will bide by the lonely lough side,
I and my merry men together.'

They built him a bothy of hazel grey,
They covered it over with heather
And there he abode till the dawn of day,
He and his merry men together.

Not an eye but his one beheld her that night,
When she called him forth from the shieling,
Not an eye beheld them – the unholy sprite,
And the Lord at her white feet kneeling.

'Swear to be mine, thou Lord of Dunluce,
Mine tonight and mine forever;
Swear to be mine thou Lord of Dunluce,
While the waters flow in Carey River.'

He swore to be hers with a terrible oath,
While water flows in Carey River;
Then she pressed his pale lips with the kiss of death,
Dunluce's Lord was hers forever!

His men wrapped his form up in cerements white,
His caoine is sung by Maev Delargey;
They carried him forth in the dead of night,
Now he rests in the bed of Margy.

And ever since then when the moon's pale rays
Look on a world in silence sleeping,
Is seen that sprite by the bosky braes,
And the Lord of Dunluce by her side a-weeping.

The Haunting of Dobbins Inn

Close to the impressive Carrickfergus Castle, there is a haunted building known as Dobbins Inn. Originally it was a family tower house built in the 1200s on land given to a Norman knight called Reginald D'Aubin. Today it is famous for the strange haunting by a seventeenth-century ghost called Maud Elizabeth Dobbins.

The family lived in the tower house for several hundred years, during which time they changed their name to Dobyn. The descendants of Reginald D'Aubin retained their importance, holding high office and being counted amongst the local dignitaries.

However, after the Gaelic chieftains were defeated and left Ireland on 4 September 1607, an event historically known as the Flight of the Earls, King James I declared that the Ulster earls were traitors to the Crown. After their flight to continental Europe, their lands and property were seized. The king decided that the only way to keep control was to 'plant' Ulster with English and Scottish settlers. Thus, in 1609, the Plantation of Ulster began and it lasted until 1690.

During this time the Catholic

Dobbins Inn.

population was under severe pressure. King James, who had been raised as a staunch Protestant, saw the Ulster Plantation as an opportunity to convert the native Irish to Protestantism. Despite the success of the plantation, James remained fearful of further uprisings and of Catholic conspiracies against him. He used this fear to justify introducing further restrictions against Catholics, including the suppression of their religion.

The Dobbin house sheltered many Catholic priests who celebrated Mass secretly around the area and were able to hide from the army in 'priest holes' and tunnels.

Around this time, Elizabeth Dobbins, the wife of a military commander stationed at Carrickfergus and owner of the house, had a passionate affair with a young soldier from the castle, affectionately known as 'Buttoncap'. At night when her husband was on duty the soldier crept through the tunnel to keep his romantic assignation with Elizabeth Maud.

Unfortunately for the couple, her husband returned earlier than expected one night and discovered his wife's adultery. According to some stories, his anger knew no bounds and he immediately 'put them to death with his sword'.

Whether he was ever punished for his crime of passion is not known, but it is said that when the neglected Dobbin House was converted into a hotel in 1946 Elizabeth Maud's ghost reappeared and to this day wanders the building. She has reportedly wakened frightened guests in the middle of the night, apparently by caressing their faces!

Other witnesses at the hotel have sworn to see her run from the reception

Blue plaque of Dobbin's Castle.

area to the stone fireplace, behind which is the entrance to the tunnel and the priests' hole. Guests have also reported dark shadows and movements and even the feeling of breath on their faces.

One guest said that she woke up one night and saw a woman sitting at a dressing table pinning up her hair. As she watched the image faltered and faded from her sight. In the morning she saw that no dressing table or stool was there, only a blank wall.

But that is not all. Dark, shadowy figures have been seen to pass right through blank walls, much to the alarm of the frightened guests. Workers in the hotel report strange occurrences – being hit by objects in empty rooms, chairs moving, and doors opening and closing by an invisible hand.

In 2011 a paranormal investigation took place and during a séance in the Thomas Seeds Room it was reported that a female energy who gave the name of Elizabeth entered the room with a palpable aura of unhappiness. Outside the room in a narrow corridor there was a distinct sound of a lady's silken dress swishing by. The paranormal investigators were absolutely certain that Dobbins Hotel was haunted.

Ghostly Lady Isabella of Ballygally

Ballygally Castle Hotel is considered one of the most haunted hotels in Ireland and it has earned its reputation from having at least four ghostly figures wandering its rooms, stairs and corridors at night. Visitors can experience 'the Ghost Room', which is said to have an eerie presence within, even though the management insists that the ghost is quite harmless and friendly.

It was built in 1625 on a promontory overlooking the quiet golden beach of Ballygally Bay, near Larne. Ballygally Head, rising 300ft above the road, is a bold feature of the scenery. On a clear day the coast of Scotland is visible.

Ballygally Castle.

Perhaps this view of his own country is what enticed James Shaw to rent the land from the Earl of Antrim for £24 a year in order to build on this stunning location.

The French-style castle has high corner turrets and a dormer window on the steep roof and with its thick walls it was capable of withstanding any attack or battle from land or sea. Shaw even had a freshwater stream flowing through the castle in case they were besieged. It seems that Shaw was determined to have a son to inherit the demesne, for over the kitchen doorway is the motto, 'God's providens is my inheritans'.

Although he may have felt nostalgia for his Scottish roots he was known to be a harsh and determined man. From all accounts it seems that he married Isabella in order to produce an heir for his fortress and lands. He was overjoyed when Isabella became pregnant but he became enraged when a baby girl was born instead of the male heir he so desperately desired.

There are several versions of the events that followed the birth. One is that he was so incensed that he snatched his newborn daughter from his wife, yelling that a baby girl was worthless and unable to inherit his estate. With a threat of revenge he locked Isabella up in a tower room. In a panicked attempt to find her daughter before harm would be done to her she tried to escape but fell to her death from the window.

Nowadays one can see that the Ghost Room in the tower is very cramped and confined and contains only a few sticks of basic furniture – a metal cot-like bed, a cabinet with mirror, a table and a portrait of a rather grim-faced woman. The one window is small but was probably large enough to allow Lady Isabella to slip through.

Another version tells us that Lady Isabella was left in the highest room in the turret to starve and although her screams echoed through the castle, the servants were forbidden to help. When Lady Isabella realised that she faced a slow lingering death now that her beautiful baby daughter was dead, she went mad and leapt to her death on the rocks below the castle walls.

A third version relates that her husband murdered Lady Isabella by pushing her to her death as she clutched her baby to her breast. Yet another version tells us that she leapt to her death to avoid having to give up her baby to her husband, who would surely kill it.

Whichever version one chooses to believe we know that Lady Isabella's ghost has wandered the castle corridors and stairs for over 400 years. She seems to tap then rap loudly on guests' doors, disturbing them in the middle of the night.

Isabella's spirit continues to haunt the narrow staircase that winds round and round as it leads up to the Ghost Room where she was held prisoner. Some have reported suddenly jerking awake in the middle of the night to see the spectre of a woman standing in their room, calling for her daughter before fading away into nothingness and leaving behind the scent of vanilla.

Others have heard distressed weeping as a woman in a white flowing garment flitted by them. Still others have reported hearing the heart-rending sobs of a baby in the vicinity of the Ghost Room. Upon investigating, the baby's screams became louder and louder until it seemed that the very walls of the staircase were filled with the echoes of distraught cries. They

followed the sounds to the Ghost Room and quietly pushed open the door. At once the crying ceased. The room was empty of people.

Another strange story was reported to have happened at Christmas some years ago. An elderly couple who arrived to stay at the hotel saw the staff attired in fancy dress and assumed that a ball had been arranged. Shortly after they retired to their room for the night a knock sounded on the door. It was one of the serving staff delivering an invitation to the ball. Although they were tired they were quite pleased with the invitation and enjoyed the most beautiful evening.

The staff and other guests all wore period costume and the couple remarked at the authenticity of the dress. When they finally went to their room the couple agreed that the ball was one of the most wonderful and unexpected evenings that they had experienced.

At breakfast the next morning they went out of their way to thank the manageress. But when she questioned the couple and listened to their description of the evening she gently told them that she was quite surprised since the ball was not due to take place for another two days. They became alarmed and checked out immediately after breakfast. Apparently this was not the first time that such a thing had happened.

But Lady Isabella is not the only ghost resident in the Ballygally Castle Hotel. The stories abound. The oldest part of the castle is said to be haunted by the ghosts of one or more children. One guest was adamant that she heard sobs and climbed the staircase; on the first-floor landing, several children were playing, but when she called to them they did not turn or

The ghost of Lady Isabella?

acknowledge her but simply disappeared.

Guests have also reported being woken up by the giggles of laughing children and little hands tugging them awake, only to find no one there, yet they heard the distinct sound of small feet running away.

A lady called Madame Nixon resided in the castle in the eighteenth century. Little is known about her. Her ghost is said to wander disconsolately around the corridors. The slight swish of her silk dress is heard, accompanied by a whiff of perfume.

In his book, *The World's Most Haunted Places*, author Jeff Belanger tells of BBC reporter Kim Lenaghan's attempt to record a piece about Ballygally Castle for the Halloween edition of *Good Morning Ulster*. She was with a psychic medium in the Ghost Room when, at the exact moment when the room became quite warm, the medium began talking to someone and a vanilla-type smell permeated the room. According to Belanger's book, 'The medium would later explain that the spirit was that of a young woman who was scared and looking for her young daughter.' The medium told Lenaghan that they were keeping her there against her will, and she said there was an older woman who wouldn't allow her to leave the room. During the conversation, this woman continually ran to the window looking for a man named Robert who was out at sea. 'The spirit couldn't understand why Robert didn't come back to get her.'

Afterwards Kim Lenaghan explained that she went back to the room and around 3 a.m. the heat rose again from no apparent source and the same vanilla smell was so all-pervasive that she ran from the room. The next morning she was confronted with the news that guests had heard loud knocking during the night and that one reported seeing a woman in her room who simply faded away. When Kim returned to the Ghost Room it was to see her name scrawled across the dusty mirror.

To this very day the ghost keeps guests awake by knocking at their bedroom doors in the middle of the night, or appearing in the room calling her daughter's name before disappearing.

The Betrayed Ghost of Carrickfergus Castle

It is no surprise that Carrickfergus Castle is rumoured to be haunted, particularly when one hears the tragic tales of love, betrayal, murder and appalling miscarriages of justice associated with it. If stones could speak what tales would the formidable walls of the castle tell? Would they tell of the headless man who walks the battlements, lamenting and calling for vengeance? With such a long and eventful past it is necessary to look at its history for some clue to explain the hauntings.

The castle has the distinction of being the oldest intact stone castle in Ireland. It is a stunning Norman fortress built

Sombre Carrickfergus Castle.

on a rocky promontory that gives it a commanding and magnificent view of Belfast Lough. This is known to be the best harbour on the north-east coast of Ulster. Historically, the castle was the stronghold of the Dalriadians and was given the name of *Carraig-Feargusa* (the rock of Fergus, after a king who was drowned there).

In 1177, Henry II gave John DeCourcy, a Norman, a grant of all the land he might conquer in Ulster. With 700 followers, DeCourcy succeeded in capturing a large part of eastern Ulster and, as was the usual Norman practice, he built the castle to rule his conquered lands.

Unfortunately, he was not popular with subsequent English kings and the castle fell into the hands of another Norman called DeLacy in 1204. DeLacy was a tyrant and his tenure did not last long before King John besieged the fortress and took control of it in 1210. He ejected DeLacy, who fled to France, but later returned by way of Scotland. There he persuaded Edward Bruce, brother of the famous Robert, to accompany him to Carrickfergus with the intention of routing the English army led by Thomas Lord Mandeville.

A bloody battle ensued followed by a second siege and Mandeville was killed. Bruce eventually secured the castle and on 6 June Edward had himself inaugurated High King of Ireland. Soon afterwards he set off for Dublin, but after several skirmishes retreated northwards again. Sir John Birmingham attacked him near Dundalk and totally routed his army, and Edward himself was killed. Meanwhile his brother Sir Robert Bruce arrived with a large army, but when he learned of Edward's fate he returned to Scotland.

Carrickfergus reverted to English control and for many years it continued to be a stronghold for them, although during the war of 1641 and the later years the fortress was alternately in the keeping of the Scots, English and Irish. In 1760, the French under the command of Commodore Thourot captured the castle, but eventually English troops rallied and the French sailed out, only to be attacked off the Isle of Man where Thourot was killed. So ended the dire expedition of the French.

About the same year, 1760, there was a soldier by the name of Robert Rainey stationed at the castle and the stories of the strange hauntings seem to emanate from his complicated love life. Rainey was known to be a womaniser and gambler who enjoyed a wild and reckless life until he fell in love. The object of his passion was a young local girl named Betsy Baird, but she refused his offer of marriage because of his reputation. He vowed that he would mend his ways and that he would be faithful to her if she would only consent to marry him. When she agreed, he was overjoyed and sang her praises far and wide.

He was unaware that Betsy was not as virginal or loyal as he had thought. She was romantically involved with the brother of his commanding officer, Colonel Jennings. When he discovered that the rumours of his fiancée's infidelity were true he flew into a state of uncontrollable rage and went in search of his rival.

As fate decreed he met him on the cliff path on his return from a clandestine tryst with Betsy. Rainey drew his sword and without giving the other man a chance to retaliate ran him through with the lethal sharp weapon. As this was the dead of night, no one witnessed his cowardly deed and he returned to his room, washed the bloodstains off his sword and his clothes and went to bed.

Colonel Jennings did not die immediately and by the time his brother reached him he was still able to describe what had happened. Unfortunately he did not identify Robert Rainey as his assailant but another young soldier, Timothy Lavery, who looked remarkably like Rainey.

This innocent young man was charged with Jennings's murder and in spite of his protestations of innocence he was sentenced to death by hanging. As the noose was placed around his neck he vowed that he would haunt the castle forever.

There is a deep, dark well in the castle around which his ghostly apparition hovers, and some call it 'Buttoncaps Well' in his honour because in life young Lavery always wore a large button in the centre of his cap. Sometimes, at night, spooked visitors to the castle have heard the cries of the distressed young man. Other witnesses have claimed to see the ghostly apparition of the innocent soldier next to the castle's wall on his knees as if begging for mercy.

Although Rainey confessed the truth many years later, Timothy Lavery's spectre seems not to have found peace in the wake of this tragic tale of betrayal by a fellow soldier. Nor could he find peace from the horrific miscarriage of justice that the guilty man had allowed to happen.

The castle remained in English hands until 1928 when it was given to the government of Northern Ireland for preservation as an ancient monument. Yet the spooky tale lives on.

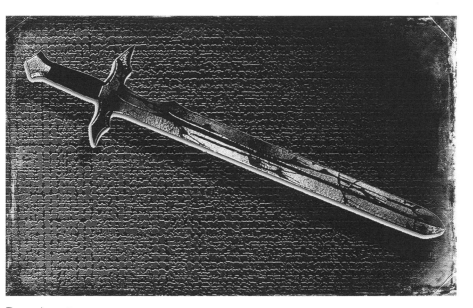

The murder weapon.

4

SINISTER PLACES AND MALIGN MANIFESTATIONS

The ABC Theatre Haunting

Deep into that darkness peering,
long I stood there wondering, fearing,
doubting, dreaming dreams
no mortal ever dared to dream before.
Edgar Allan Poe, 'The Raven'

Jim McNeill, who tells the following story, was the under-manager in the ABC Cinema on Great Victoria Street in Belfast. Formerly known as the Ritz, it was one of the most popular cinemas in the city. It was a beautiful theatre, the biggest in Northern Ireland at the time, with an organ in the pit and a grand piano on the big stage for the live shows. It had a capacity for 2,200 people and had over 60 members of staff, all of whom wore a uniform.

At the time of this eerie happening, Nigel Empett, an Englishman, was the manager and Mr Brown was the assistant manager.

Jim recalls, 'I moved there, as the junior assistant manager and I loved it. Just to work in a place like that was a marvelous experience. Back in the 1960s, it showed classic films like *Gone with the Wind* as well as modern ones like *2001, A Space Odyssey*.

'When I started there Nigel took me to one side on the first day I was there and said to me,

'"Jim, after the show is over you will have to count all the takings from the box-office and make sure that it balances with the ticket sales and so forth. If it tallies, you must then lock everything away in the safe. When you are working at night after the show, don't stay here by yourself."

'I thought that a bit strange and asked why, but Nigel simply added, "Make sure that the doorman or one of the staff is in the building too."

'It crossed my mind that they were trying to spook me or trying to do something funny, maybe play a trick on

ABC cinema.

me but they wouldn't explain. Anyway, one night I had to stay late because we were having a roadshow on. After it was over, I was counting the money but it wasn't balancing out right. I had to recount it and it was taking longer. All the staff had gone home except Jimmy Black, the chief doorman. Time was running on and I had to call my girlfriend Anne, who lived about 15 minutes away to let her know I would be late because I usually met her after work.

'I called Jimmy and told him to go on home because I wasn't sure when I'd be finished.

'He said, "Oh no, Mr McNeill, I have to stay, you aren't to be here on your own."

'But I persuaded him and eventually I got the takings to balance about midnight. All the managers then wore tuxedos at the front of the house so I had to walk back through the theatre to the dressing rooms to change out of my tuxedo into my street clothes.

'There were quite a few dressing rooms at the back for the big names like the Beatles, the Rolling Stones, the Bee Gees and Englebert Humperdink, who all came to play in the theatre when we had a week-long stage show.

'I headed for the managers' dressing room to change. There were three washrooms in the same area and Nigel had told me to leave the light on there because the window could be seen from the street. Apparently when the police drove around at night, once they saw the light on it was a signal that everything was okay. He'd told me to make sure I didn't turn the light off. I thought that was a clever idea so was careful to leave it on.

'For some reason, I looked back to the washroom and the light was off even though I was sure it had been left on. But I thought maybe I was mistaken and I turned back, switched on the light and walked away leaving the door open. As I hurried back down the corridor towards the exit, the washroom door slammed shut. I jumped as the sound echoed around the empty theatre but I went back thinking that there must be a draught from a window or something. I opened the door and the light was out. I was puzzled. I turned on the light and checked the window and it was closed.

'A strange feeling came over me. I knew I wasn't imagining things so I called, "Is anybody there?" I looked in the stalls in the theatre too because we had to make sure that the theatre was empty before we left at night but I couldn't see anyone there so I went back, feeling quite nervous and I yelled louder, "Is somebody there?"

'I checked the washroom again and noticed that it was getting quite cold, frigid actually, and I was really nervous at this time. I switched on the light again, left the door open and walked quickly down the hallway. I was sure in my mind that as I walked away the door would slam again and sure enough that is what it did. I decided I'd try it once again. The door was definitely closed and when I turned the handle, it turned all right, but the door did not open. I began pushing but it was as if someone was on the other side pushing against it to keep me from going in. It wouldn't open and I shouted once again, "Is anybody there?" Only silence answered me.

'I thought, "I'm going out of my mind here!" I hurried back down to my office and decided to call my girlfriend, Anne Shepherd.

'"Look, Anne," I said, "I know it's late but could you come down here and bring your father with you because there's something strange going on and I don't know what it is."

'I went on to explain to her that I didn't want the police to call the manager in the middle of the night when they didn't see the light on.

'A short time later Anne came down with her daddy and she had her little poodle, Silver, with her. Although he was a small dog he absolutely feared nothing. Anyway, I brought them up through the theatre and across the balcony on the way to my office. To get there we had to pass the washrooms but as soon as the dog came to the stairs into the balcony it froze, it was scared. Its hackles rose and it backed off. That was really spooky because we'd never seen the dog like that before. Anne and her dad remarked how cold it was as we walked up the stairs. When we reached the washroom the same thing happened again and it shocked them. This weird thing really was happening. I felt relieved because I knew then that it wasn't just my over-active imagination. And I thought, "It's not me. I'm not crazy."

'I realised that I would have to call the police to tell them and they came very quickly. They searched the whole building until about three in the morning but the only thing they found was a water tap running in one of the dressing rooms, as if someone had been interrupted washing himself. The police were adamant that there was definitely no one anywhere in the theatre and they left.

'The next day I told Nigel and he said, "That's the reason I told you never to stay here by yourself. This theatre is haunted."

'I was still a bit skeptical and although I knew there was something strange going on, I replied, "Haunted? Honestly!"

'He assured me that it was, "but don't tell anyone about it because the bad publicity will damage sales."

'In the summer of 1968 we were advertising the movies to get people in. The ABC managers in England would award us points towards company prizes for managers, depending on the publicity and other things. We were always thinking of ways to say, get an article in the newspaper or publicity on the radio for the upcoming films.

'There was one made by Hammer Films called *The Devil Rides Out*, based on a Denis Wheatley novel by the same name and directed by Terence Fisher. Denis Wheatley was a known Satanist and apparently in the book on which the film was based the actual words for calling up the devil were used.

'I had read some articles about the making of the movie and it seems there were some inexplicable accidents, apparently even someone died during the making of the movie. The director changed the words for calling up the devil but the general reviews labeled it a Satanist shocker.

'When Nigel asked me what we should do to publicise the film, I admit that I was a bit nervous but suggested that we could invite someone to sit through the movie at midnight. So we arranged that the newspapers should do articles to help promote the film. *The Devil Rides Out* with Christopher Lee starring was to be the main feature and the second one was *The Blood Beast Terror* with Peter Cushing. I'd voiced my concerns to Nigel saying that I didn't like the idea of a Satanist movie being shown

The Devil Rides Out *film poster.*

in a place that was supposedly haunted. He partly agreed with me but Nigel was an atheist and thought that I was being a superstitious Irish man. So in the end we agreed to try it.

'The *Belfast Telegraph* and *The Irish News* wrote articles asking if anyone would be brave enough to sit through the film on their own at midnight on the Friday before the movie opened to the general public. We interviewed some people and there was a girl of sixteen I think, who said she would do it.

'She was a Goth; you know the style where they dressed all in black with heavy whitish makeup and black eye makeup. We chose her and when the night of the showing came a reporter and a photographer from the *Belfast Telegraph* were there. We arranged to show it after the regular show that evening.

'When this girl came in we told her that she would be sitting upstairs in the balcony and she would be the only one in the whole theatre but that she would have a buzzer, which would be connected to the projection room. If she became too frightened she could press the buzzer and the projectionist would stop the film. We said she could have anything she wanted from the snack bar, which had all sorts of expensive things like huge boxes of chocolates, caramel popcorn, etc., but all she wanted were two packets of Rowntrees Fruit Gums. I found that amusing.

'Once she had those we brought her up to the balcony. It was big and she sat roughly in the middle. The photographer took pictures and left. Then the reporter came down and sat with me in the middle of the stalls underneath the balcony but we didn't let her know that we were there. I was in the middle of the row, the reporter was on my left and Nigel was at the end of the row.

'The movie started and the first fifteen minutes were slow but I could see that Nigel was quite nervous and he rose and went back a few times. When he sat down he kept looking to the back of the stalls towards the exit sign above the door. He rose another time and left and I looked after him. In the light of the doorway I saw that he seemed to be looking for somebody. He did not seem to see the large black shadow right beside him sort of crouched over, not touching him but certainly leaning over. To me it seemed to be a tall man, yet Nigel still appeared to be looking for something, unaware of the shadow even though it was beside him. Then he left the auditorium.

'Just after that I could hear some clicking noises that seemed to come from the carpeted floor and I thought that it was the photographer coming back to the theatre to scare his friend the reporter. I assumed that the clicking noises were from his camera. I thought that I'd play along with his trick and didn't look back anymore.

'Then I heard someone come down the aisle and the seat right behind me went down and someone sat in it. I could hear him breathing and I kept looking across at the reporter but he didn't seem to notice anything. I could still hear the clicking noise and breathing. I was thinking that the photographer was waiting for me to leave so that he could scare his friend all the more. I was half prepared for him to jump and shout but if he did, I would certainly jump too.

'As I got up to check with Nigel I turned around and saw the seat was still down and those seats do not stay down

unless there is a weight on them. But the seat was empty; there was no one there. I knew that was impossible. My legs went like jelly. I moved but I could hardly walk up the aisle to the exit I was so frightened. Then I began to get a bit angry thinking, "What the heck is going on there? Is someone trying to scare me?"

'I made my way out through the foyer, and ran up the set of stairs to the office. I was still angry and thought I'd give Nigel a piece of my mind; after all he was the manager. At the top I could see that his office door was open and when I went in he was standing at his desk. He was as white as a ghost and I said, "What the hell is going on here? Who was that man?"

'He said, "What man?"

'I was so annoyed and answered, "Don't fool with me! Who was that man? You must have seen him. He was crouched down beside you. What is going on? Something is happening here." I was getting angrier.

'He looked at me, "You've heard something too, haven't you?"

'"Heard what," I demanded.

'He said, "There is something going on but it's not me, Jim."

'Nigel told me that the reason he looked back and kept getting up from his seat was that he thought that someone had come in.

'At that moment there was a terrible ear-piercing scream from above. I turned to rush up the other flight of stairs to the balcony to see if the girl was all right but Nigel ran after me and grabbed my arm.

'"It's the film, Jim, it's not the girl. Don't go in there."

'But I heard another scream and rushed up into the balcony. There was no screaming coming from the screen. Then

I heard another moaning sort of scream coming from the middle of the balcony but I couldn't see the girl. I ran to where I thought she was but Nigel shouted, 'Don't go, she would have pressed the buzzer.'

'Just after that the buzzer sounded and the lights went on. I ran over and the girl was there, crouched down in her seat. I can honestly say that I have never seen anyone so scared in my life. She was trembling and terrified and crying uncontrollably.

'We said, "What's wrong?"

'She said, "Something came right behind me and was breathing on me and all I could hear were clicking noises."

'I asked, "Why didn't you press the buzzer?"

'She said, "I was so frightened I couldn't move. I tried but I couldn't and then I dropped the buzzer."

'We helped her down to the office and let her talk a bit until she calmed down. After that we went down to the lobby to the reporter. He had heard nothing other than her screaming. Rather than stay in the theatre we walked to a local hotel to talk it over. Nigel, without much persuasion, divulged what had happened to him previous to this when he took over the theatre.

'He said that there were times at night when the building became really cold at particular places, one of them being where the stairs led up to the balcony. The usherettes who showed people to their seats refused to stand there because there was such a strange sensation of cold and unease at that spot.

'The sales girls refused to go down the left-hand side of the theatre after nine o'clock because they said that they felt an invisible presence, something pushing them out of the way as if it was running past.

'Pauline Short, the lady who worked the Concessions Stand told me later that they had seen a man in black always rushing down the left-hand side of the auditorium and that the smell of perfume was at times overpowering and there was no obvious explanation.

'She didn't want to scare the girls any further so did not tell them of these strange goings-on but they confessed that they did not like to stand at those points of the theatre because it was creepy, cold and really scary. Later I found out that they had been told not to speak of any of this because it would be bad publicity.

'Nigel explained that he was in the theatre one night when *My Fair Lady* was showing and they had mannequins in the lobby for a display. They were wearing dresses, replicas of Audrey Hepburn's that she'd worn in the film. Nigel stayed on late to count the tickets and within seconds his office became exceptionally cold and a strong smell of perfume pervaded the air.

'He continued, "I thought that someone went into the ladies' washroom near the balcony and I followed but when I opened the door there was no one there. When I left and walked away I heard the washroom door squeak open again behind me and then slam shut. I returned to the lobby but it was ice-cold too and unbelievably the mannequins had been knocked down to the floor and dragged across the lobby. One dress, the copy of Audrey Hepburn's, was ripped to shreds and that must have happened in a matter of seconds." He called the manager from the *News and Cartoon Theatre* across the road and asked him to come over so that he could see and verify what had happened.

'One night another eerie thing happened on the big stage. A grand piano sat at the side and it was dragged from one end of the stage to the other although no one was there.

'Nigel asked the reporter not to publish what had occurred on the night of the showing of *The Devil Rides Out* because they were so concerned that people would not come to the theatre if they knew it was haunted. The strange thing is that the reporter was aware of nothing until he heard the screams of the girl, yet Nigel and I heard everything.

'The reporter did look into things and it appears that the Ritz Cinema (as it was called then) was opened in 1936 and previous to that there was always a fair and he said that a man and woman were both killed on that site where the theatre was built. He surmised that because they had a violent death their spirits were unsettled and for some reason still lingered there.

'One of the most frightening experiences for me was the knowledge that once we left the hotel where we had discussed things, we had to go back into the theatre to change out of our tuxedos. Going up to the balcony and through it to the corridor where the washrooms and dressing rooms were almost made me sick with fear. The place was freezing cold inside even though it was mild weather outside. The hair on the back of my head was standing up and Nigel said, "I thought when I came here that it was just you superstitious Irish but I have to say, Jim, that there is something in this theatre and it is evil."

'We managed to get changed and out of the theatre without further incident that night but I'll never forget it nor do I want to experience it again. Maybe that satanic film brought the presence out more forcefully than before but I wish we had never shown it.'

(Denis Wheatley was a British author and a professed Satanist was best known for his black-magic tales. He collected occult esoterica. It seems he was delighted with the film, particularly as Matheson's script had expanded on his own research into black-magic rituals, legends, occult and pagan texts.)

The Blacksmiths and the Ghost

Randalstown in the late 1700s and early 1800s was just a small village in County Antrim. The story goes that a blacksmith called James Walker lived there and he was known to be one of the most skilled in the area. Everyone considered him an honest and industrious man who attended his Presbyterian church regularly. If occasionally he took a little too much to drink his friends and customers generally turned a blind eye because of his pleasant demeanour and excellent workmanship.

Another blacksmith, by the name of Harry O'Donnell, lived about a mile and a half from the village on the road to Ahoghill. Harry was very like James in many respects and he also enjoyed drinking the 'mountain dew' to quench his thirst. As he was wont to say, 'Sure only a jug of punch can soften the spark in the throat caused by sweating over the roaring fire in the forge and hammering red-hot iron on the anvil.'

There was one difference though: James was often seen to be a little tipsy on a Sunday but Harry was careful never to be seen the worse for wear especially when he passed through Randalstown on the Sabbath.

At any other time though when Harry came to the village the two of them enjoyed sharing a 'drop' together. When they met in the tavern they had a firm rule never to discuss the sacred subject of religion over a drink. Instead they freely discussed the tricks of their trade, whether it was the shoeing of horses, the making of spades or other ironmongery related to what farmers in the area needed. In doing that they helped each other to improve their smithying, at least that was their excuse for a day's drinking.

One autumn Harry was busy getting the corn stored and the potatoes in the pit before the frost set in and so he delayed seeing his friend. Once he finished the farm work he resolved to visit James and since he was heading into Randalstown he would use the trip to buy some more iron and other things

he needed. As soon as that business was taken care of, he and James would share a bottle and drink to each other's health.

It was a dreary afternoon when Harry bade goodbye to his family, telling them not to worry if he was late home because he was sure to have some company on the way back. He was in a happy frame of mind as he walked along swinging his hawthorn stick and admiring the countryside around. He didn't feel the time passing and soon he reached Randalstown. Once he bought the things he needed he called at James's forge and received a warm welcome and a little admonishment for not visiting more often.

James donned his winter coat and they hurried to the Black Bull tavern. There, the landlord showed them to a quiet little parlour where a warm turf fire glowed in the grate. They were served a jug of warm punch that disappeared quickly as they chatted about their usual topics. The

The blacksmith's anvil.

landlord kept refilling the jug and before they knew it, it was nearly time for them to be on their way. Harry remarked that he would have to pass the Drumarory Bush on his way home and this led to a discussion on that famous hawthorn, known to be the haunt of fairies, witches and ghosts.

'Even the devil himself was seen there,' whispered Harry, 'and sure, I'm not telling you a word of a lie when I say that I'm *afeard* to walk past there on my own.'

This led to a discussion – and another naggin of punch – about the alarming things that had happened there, with James protesting that there were no such things as fairies or ghosts or the like. Finally, though, he saw that Harry could not be convinced and promised to accompany him past the hawthorn bush.

Needless to say, Harry was delighted and relieved that he would not be on his own should anything unusual happen.

Having sorted the return journey out, the two men went to the bar to pay their bill and when they were offered another naggin they sat down once again at the fire where the assembled drinkers plied them with questions until finally the two men were hardly able to keep their eyes open. However, eventually they said their goodbyes and staggered off. As they approached the Drumarory Bush James was still protesting his disbelief in the ghostly world and singing, 'What dreaded bush was drawing nigh, what ghosts and witches nightly cry.'

Everything seemed quiet but they had scarcely taken another couple of steps when the bright glare of a light sprang up out of nowhere and seemed to dance around the bush rapidly swinging from side to side.

The dancing light.

The two blacksmiths stopped abruptly and suddenly a white spectre appeared on the road in front of them and gave a wild unearthly scream. And when they turned to run away another scream split the air beside them.

James's bravado left him and the two men took to their heels to run the half-mile back to the town. Harry glanced around and saw the white ghost and the light following them. Then when they came to Feehoge Avenue the ghostly light and apparition glided down a dark road and disappeared. Breathless and in shock the blacksmiths slowed down to catch their breath but their terror was not over. There was the sound of footsteps approaching behind them and they were poised to run again when they heard a frightened voice cry out, 'If you are Christians or men, I entreat you to stand for I am frightened out of my life by a ghost.'

They turned and saw that the man was the Randalstown barber, a Mr Jamie Irons, who seemed ready to faint. Harry suggested they return to the Black Bull for a glass of whiskey to settle their nerves.

There, they related what had happened to them and were backed up by the barber's story – he said that when he was coming up Feehoge Avenue, a ghost in white, possibly a woman, followed by a blazing light, passed him and glided through the nearby orchard hedge without stopping of making a sound. The outcome of all of this in the tavern was more drink and more and more questions.

Only when the flow of whiskey dried up did Jamie Irons suggest that they could see Harry safely past the Drumarory Bush and off they set. When they approached that part the only sound was that of the nearby River Main, although all three kept looking around afraid of a repetition of the earlier manifestation.

Once they reached the top of Drumarory Brae Harry scampered off home safely leaving James and Jamie to return to Randalstown, which they did without incident.

As you might guess the two black-smiths swore never to stay so late in the tavern until the light days of summer were upon them – at least that's how the story goes!

Cavehill's Ghost Traveller

In the 1950s few people could afford to go abroad on holiday so cycling and camping were in great vogue. People left Belfast and cycled to the seaside or to the hills surrounding the city of Belfast. Cavehill was very popular and the route by Hightown Road leading onto the Horseshoe Road saw plenty of people folk especially at holiday time. Most were prepared for the inconsistency of the weather but not all came with the proper gear to withstand storms. A group of young men set up camp at the back of Cavehill thinking that if the weather changed they could find shelter in one of the caves.

It was a quiet starry night and they sat around the campfire toasting sausages and bread and telling stories. Being young and strong they considered themselves brave enough to sleep in the open under the stars but they made a rule that they wouldn't tell ghost stories.

Hardly had they settled down but the weather broke and they made a beeline for an old dilapidated cottage a few hundred yards away. Although it was in a bad shape it was at least dry. Once inside they settled down to sleep again.

Sometime near midnight, just outside the house, the sound of a horse and cart and the loud voice of the driver egging the horse to gallop faster woke up the young men. At the time they paid no heed for the sound faded away and they went back to sleep not waking until around dawn.

One of the boys ventured outside and saw a farmhouse fairly close by. He assumed that the cottage where they slept belonged to the farmer so he headed off in that direction to let him know that they had taken advantage of the shelter and hopefully get some milk and bread.

The farmer's wife was welcoming and plied him with as much as he could carry, telling him that he and the others were welcome to stay in the old house if they wished.

By way of conversation the lad asked about the horse and cart they'd heard the previous night. She seemed a little startled and answered briskly that gypsies often stayed in their far field and it had probably been them. He accepted her explanation but when he looked back he saw the woman speaking to a man whom he took to be her husband. He appeared angry and was gesticulating and looking in his direction and although the boy could not hear the actual words being shouted he assumed the man was objecting to their stay in the old house.

The other three lads had a pot boiling in the old grate and were delighted with the food. As they ate the boy who had fetched the food asked if they wanted to stay there for another night or head off somewhere else. All voted to stay and the hope was that the farmer wouldn't make too much of a fuss.

So, they climbed to the summit of Cavehill and passed a very pleasant day before returning to the old cottage. It was dusk and for a moment it seemed that a light shone from the broken window but it disappeared before they entered. All four quietly put the illumination down to the moon that was now beginning to rise.

Like the previous night, they lay down exhausted from the day's rambling and climbing and hoping for a good night's sleep. Outside the wind began to rise and the old door loose on its hinges started rattling. Rain pattered on the tin roof and the temperature in the room suddenly dropped until it was almost freezing. By now all of them were awake and they blamed the storm for not being able to sleep. The youngest took out his harmonica and started to play to relieve the tension that each of them felt. They chatted and sang quietly until the sound of hooves galloping heavily on the gravel outside brought them to an uneasy silence. They looked at each other, clearly frightened.

A mighty shout echoed, 'Get up there, ye lazy animal', and the crack of a whip ripped through the air. Unlike on the previous night, the only noise they heard now was the whinnying of a horse. But then heavy footsteps approached the house. The door that had been hanging on one hinge was pushed open and the wind and rain rushed in but no one entered. And now there came a rattling cough and wheezing breath and it seemed as if a dark shadow was passing by.

After a few seconds, which seemed like an hour to the four young men, the door swung crazily on its hinge again and with another crack of the whip and coarse swear words, the pounding of

Was this a ghostly manifestation or imagination?

horses' hooves and cart wheels gradually faded. Yet when two of the lads went outside there was nothing, not even the trace of tracks on the wet grass.

There was no sleep for the youths for the rest of that night and at the crack of dawn they went to the farm. The farmer was already working in the field and as they approached he straightened up.

'Aye,' he said, 'what have ye come to tell me?'

They related the happenings of the previous night in a garbled way and the farmer simply nodded his head.

'I told the wife not to let you stay because it's not the first time that has happened. Why do you think we moved out of there to here? Sure that whole house and yard is haunted and nothing will rid it of its burden. I heard tell that, before we went to live there, a gypsy family tried the settled life there because the wife couldn't stick the travelling. But he was a thick sort of a man and kept telling her they were going to move on. Sure when he came home one evening with a cart ready to pack up she was already gone, nobody knows where to. What did he do but hang himself in there? Leastways that's the story that was told to me so if I were you I'd be on my way.'

The boys packed up and left in a mighty hurry and it wasn't until many years later that the story came out.

Devil Worship at Crebilly

On 23 March 1990, a strange story made headlines in the *Ballymena Times*.

According to the reporter, a young photography student, Ken Allen, from the local technical college was searching for abandoned houses to photograph. His eye caught a derelict cottage at Crebilly, which lies on the outskirts of Ballymena.

He approached the house on his bicycle and began to photograph the door but he became aware of a terrible smell emanating from the house. He crept inside and what he saw made him rush to the door for fresh air.

'It was the remains of a chicken that looked as if it had been ripped apart.'

The young student hurriedly left.

He was aware that stories were circulating about 'devil worship' in the Ballymena area so he visited the offices of the aforesaid newspaper. A reporter went with him to the house and although slogans were painted on the inside walls they seemed to have been painted some time before and the slogans didn't seem to relate to the sinister evidence that the two found when they explored further.

Lying on the ground was a fundamentalist tract which contained graphic depictions of murder, Satanic sacrifice and a frightening portrait of the Earth being destroyed by 'fire and brimstone'. The pamphlet had a drawing of people seemingly taking part in the Black Arts, declaring, 'I've come to worship you my Lord Satan', and 'Tonight he will bring forth the Prince of Darkness'.

Lying, as it was, near a dismembered chicken, it seemed to suggest demonic activity that many local evangelists claimed took place there. The tract was one from the Book of Revelations, which is often studied by Satanists.

Some time after that a woman said that she had driven by the house late one night and slowed down when she saw a light flickering through the window aperture. When she turned her head again to the road she had to brake suddenly because a tall man dressed in dark clothes had appeared right in

Did Satanic worship take place here?

Sacrificial chicken.

front of the car. At first she thought it was someone who wanted to warn her about the road ahead but then she saw 'red burning eyes' in what she described as a wolf's face. She screamed and the face shimmered before her and for one terrifying moment she felt paralysed by fear. As the figure approached she pressed her foot on the accelerator and the car leapt forward, straight towards the dark form.

It bounded away but not before she saw that it wasn't human. It was like an animal that she had never seen before. Was this perhaps some devil apparition?

George 'Bloody' Hutchinson's Ghost

The story goes that on All Hallow's Eve George 'Bloody' Hutchinson's ghost haunts the Main Street of Ballymoney.

The derogatory title 'Bloody' comes from Hutchinson's merciless actions against the United Irishmen.

He lived in Stranocum Hall, which was built by his ancestors in the eighteenth century and they lived there until 1848. Their ancestry can be traced back to William Hutchinson who settled in the small village of Stranocum about 5 miles north-west of Ballymoney in 1598.

The Hutchinson brothers, Richard and George, served as officers in the Dunluce Yeomanry Corps loyal to King George III. At that time there was widespread disillusionment amongst both Presbyterians and Catholics who were barred from voting because they did not pass a property threshold. The king and the parliament governed Ireland and had the power to veto any Irish legislation and also to legislate for the whole kingdom.

The United Irishmen wanted to achieve reform and greater autonomy from Britain. This prospect of reform inspired a small group of Protestant liberals in Belfast to found the Society of United Irishmen in 1791. The organisation crossed the religious divide with Presbyterian, Catholic, Methodist and other Protestant dissenting members. Even some people from the Protestant Ascendancy joined the ranks. The society was very clear that its aim was to further the cause of democratic reforms and Catholic Emancipation, which the Irish parliament had little intention of granting.

While George and Richard Hutchinson were on duty with the Yeomanry on the night of 8 June, United Irishmen attacked Richard's home, Stranocum Hall. They took a hostage, James Crosbie, one of Richard's servants, and brought him to their camp. Not content with that, they stole one of Richard's horses for their commander to ride as he led them to Ballymena to join other rebel forces.

The rebellion failed and all the known rebels were arrested. Hutchinson was a local magistrate and as such was encouraged to hand down harsh punishments like public lashings, transportation to the penal colonies or hanging for those more deeply involved. Hutchinson showed no mercy towards those whom he blamed for the loss of life and property. Some say that his merciless sentences were driven more by vengeance against the people who dared attack his home than by justice.

To this day he is infamous for his actions. Legend tells us that he took personal pride in the number of rebels he sentenced to death following the United Irish Rebellion of 1798. He sentenced two men at Dungorbery and ordered them to be hanged from a tree on the top of a hill. It is assumed that two bodies unearthed 50 years later at that site were these two men.

One of Hutchinson's most brutal and contentious acts was the hanging of Alexander Gamble, who was tried and hanged at the clock tower at the top of Main Street in Ballymoney. Hutchinson apparently demanded that he inform on his fellow United Irishmen and tried to bribe him by sparing his life if he did so. It is reported that his answer was, 'I will die some day, and know not when; but it will never be cast in the face of my children that their father betrayed others to save himself.'

The Crown retaliated against the so-called rebels and traitors by burning down much of the town of Ballymoney. This was on the flimsiest evidence that it was, by and large, a rebel stronghold. Although George Hutchinson's house was destroyed he received a goodly sum of compensation in return.

It is believed that his spirit does not rest easy in the graveyard beside the old church tower, for legend has it that it manifests itself at midnight on every Friday the thirteenth. With a large metal ball chained to his ankle, George 'Bloody' Hutchinson limps his way down the Main Street before turning back again. Some people say that his spirit will disappear forever if he can be prevented from completing his journey. As yet, no one has been foolhardy enough to try. Although some of the locals say that on one occasion a man, drunk enough to accept the challenge to spend the night in the graveyard, appeared the next morning naked, his hair having turned white, speaking gibberish about the 'ghosts'.

Haunted Crumlin Road Jail

Crumlin Road Jail is a sombre building at the bottom of the Crumlin Road. With its black basalt exterior one can easily imagine that it now houses ghosts as it once housed prisoners.

It was designed by Sir Charles Lanyon and built at a cost of £60,000 to replace the county jail for Antrim, which was located in Carrickfergus. It was considered a model prison when it was finished in 1846 and in that same year the first 106 prisoners were marched in chains from the old jail to the new one.

Shamefully, many of the prisoners were impoverished women and children sentenced for stealing food or clothing. This was the time of the famine in Ireland and thousands of people were dying of starvation.

Although the prison was built to accommodate only 300 prisoners, more were sentenced and it rapidly became overcrowded. Discipline was harsh, food scarce and only the strongest were fit enough to survive. One of the prisoners was a 13-year-old boy, Patrick Magee, who was sentenced to 3 months, but unfortunately never completed his sentence. Instead, unable to bear the cruel regime, he hanged himself in his cell in 1858. His spirit was said to be heard weeping in the night. A prisoner who was incarcerated in the same cell in which Patrick had languished begged to be moved to another cell, such was the deep sadness that enveloped him there.

Many other prisoners suffered great indignities in that place, including the Ulster Suffragettes, Dorothy Evans and Madge Muir, who were incarcerated in 1914 for arson and possession of explosives. When they went on hunger strike they were force-fed until they became ill. They were released under the Cat and Mouse Act (once they got well they would be incarcerated again) but they drove around Belfast in a car festooned with Suffragette flags. So Crumlin Road Jail was a place that knew defiance and punishment.

Crumlin Road Jail.

It also knew the imprisonment and death of seventeen men who were hanged there. Before this prison was built, executions were carried out in public open spaces, but the new jail had a special execution cell designed only for hangings. It also had an underground tunnel leading from the courthouse that faced it across the Crumlin Road, so no prisoner had to face the public who were often hostile because they were deprived of the spectacle of a hanging.

One man in particular is thought to be the ghost that haunts this execution room and corridor leading to it. The man protested his innocence even as he walked to the gallows. His name was Eddie Cullens and he was the only Jew as well as being the only American to be hanged in Crumlin Jail.

The evidence offered was circumstantial but it was enough for the jury to convict him of the murder of Achmet Musa, a Turkish circus worker who lived in Carrickfergus. Although Cullens was a naturalised American citizen, he was a native of Smyrna in western Turkey. He, Musa and two others were involved in touring with a travelling circus and when they arrived in Belfast Cullens and Musa stayed in Ryan's Hotel in Donegall Quay in Belfast. Cullens insisted that the three of them went to see some dog racing in Celtic Park and that Musa went missing.

Cullens travelled to Liverpool and thence to London where he was subsequently arrested for the murder, which he strenuously denied. No motive for the murder was ever established but after a trial of three days the jury found him guilty on the flimsiest of circumstantial evidence. He spoke from the dock, saying, 'All I can say is that when I spoke my oath yesterday that I was not guilty it

The execution cell.

was the Gospel truth.'

Although the date of the hanging was set for 29 December 1931, Cullens lodged an appeal for mercy and his request to introduce new evidence was denied. The Crown dismissed the appeal and the execution took place on 13 January 1932.

On 16 January 1932 the *Weekly Northern Whig* newspaper reported that:

Eddie Cullens, the American Jew, was executed in Belfast Prison for the murder of Achmet Musa, the Turk, near Carrickfergus, in September last. During Cullens' confinement he acted calmly, talked freely to the warders and ate well and on Wednesday morning walked calmly to the scaffold.

He had slept fairly well during the night, and about six o'clock was wakened by the warders. He had a little breakfast, and maintained his composure till the end.

Rabbi Shacter, who attended him on the morning of his execution, told the *Belfast Telegraph* that Cullens 'went to the scaffold with the deep conviction that his hands were clean and clear of the blood of Musa'.

Shortly after Eddie Cullens was hanged several prison officers saw his ghost. On the morning of his execution, when he was standing on the scaffold, another prison officer swore that a man who appeared out of nowhere right in front of him in the corridor that led to the execution room was Eddie. He gazed at the officer and disappeared after a few seconds, leaving the officer frightened and uneasy.

That was not the end of the appearances. Shortly after that some of the prisoners were confronted by the same spectre of a man at the other side of the corridor. The prisoners and the officer were adamant that it was the ghost of Eddie Cullens they had seen.

The sightings have continued and visitors often remark on the cold eerie feeling that they experience in that corridor. Is this his spirit that haunts Crumlin Road Jail?

In the year 2000, the Royal Prerogative of Mercy was exercised to enable the removal of the bodies of those interred within the grounds of the jail should a relative wish to claim them for reburial. No one came forward to claim that of Eddie Cullen. The exact location is not known so his stay at the jail will continue, but even though his body is interred, his spirit seems to roam free.

The Ghostly Gallop of Squire O'Hara

'Words have no power to impress the mind
Without the exquisite horror of their reality.'

Edgar Allan Poe

Ghostly appearances on particular nights of the year hold a sinister fascination, and one such disturbing manifestation takes place in Ballymarlow Graveyard on Christmas Eve.

On the stroke of twelve midnight, Squire O'Hara, the last squire of Crebilly Castle near Ballymena, gallops from the graveyard to the Kennel Bridge. He has been seen whipping his white horse almost to a frenzy until the froth foams from its mouth, as he pushes it to jump the white gates of the castle. The squire does not relent and drives his mount to the bridge to make a tremendous leap over it towards the water below. As soon as the horse's white tail disappears from sight an eerie silence follows. There is no sound of a splash, as one would expect when it hits the water. There is a very good reason for the unearthly stillness. Both horse and rider have disappeared into the darkness of the supernatural.

The dissolute Henry Hamilton O'Hara would seem to have taken after his father John Francis O'Hara, who was spoken of as a blackguard and a rake of the worst kind in eighteenth-century Ireland.

Henry Hamilton and the white gates of Crebilly.

In 1786, John Francis was a bachelor living at Crebilly but that did not prevent him from answering an advertisement in a Dublin newspaper. A young French girl who sought to work as a governess or companion for a gentleman's family placed the advertisement. The squire corresponded with her and offered her the position in his home.

She arrived, expecting to meet his wife and children, but to her dismay she realised that she had been duped. The frightened girl, Mademoiselle Madeleine Collett, fled to the house of the parish priest and, with what little English she had, stuttered out her dilemma.

The priest was appalled and set off on horseback to confront the squire who, it appeared, acted in a reasonable manner, and although he was not exactly the sort of person the girl would have chosen herself, she agreed when the priest related what Squire John Francis had suggested, that she should become his wife. She had no other option open to her in that strange country, and the priest performed the rite of marriage in Crebilly Castle's drawing room there and then. The marriage remained to be legally solemnised in law, so the squire arranged that they would go to Scotland and there the marriage was witnessed and legalised.

Within two years, their first son was born but the local people were wary and somewhat suspicious of a lady who spoke their language with a strange accent. They called her Madame O'Hara. This annoyed the squire, but soon he too began to find fault with his young wife. He schemed to rid himself of her and did so in an underhand way. When she was expecting their second child, he arranged that they should go to London for the birth. He put his wife on board a boat at Donaghadee to sail to Port Patrick, whence she would travel by coach to London while he would supposedly follow via Dublin where he purported to have some business.

He never came nor did he send any money to her to support their second child Claude, who was born shortly after her arrival in London. She was reduced to earning a living by dress-making for the rich ladies of the town but the pittance that she earned was barely enough to live on.

Eventually some friends persuaded him to travel to London but on the way he connived a plot to rid himself of her for good. He forced her to sign a prom-issory note for the money he gave her and to give up her rights to their elder child. Of course, she had no idea of the contents of the note, which stated also that she had to pay back the money with interest.

O'Hara was well acquainted with the law and put his scheme into action by deliberately making out the note in her maiden name of Collett and not her legal name of O'Hara. He waited some months until the money became due and when the date arrived and no money was forthcoming, as he had planned, he had her arrested and thrown into Newgate Prison for 'bad debt'.

She languished there for 8 months before he relented and paid the debt himself. But he played the same dastardly trick again and this time she was imprisoned in Marshalsea Prison. Her fate from then on is unknown.

He had a clear field now to wed and bed the niece of Lord O'Neill but that was a failure almost from the start and already he was looking around for a third wife. His eye fell on the daughter of the yardman, 18-year-old Eliza Duffin, and there was a riotous feast on the wedding night culminating in a huge bonfire on Pigeon Hill.

It seems that this marriage was more successful than the two previous ones because Eliza gave birth to two children, Henry Hamilton and Mary. However, John Francis O'Hara died while Henry was still a boy and left the valuable legacy of the estate of Crebilly worth £40,000 (about £1.5 million in today's value) plus an annual rent of over £1,000, which was held in trust until Henry came of age.

But Henry Hamilton was not as miserly as his father, although he was every bit as dissolute. It would appear that the 'bad blood' was passed from father to son. He went to Cambridge and ran up mountainous gambling debts so that by the time he returned to Crebilly the estate was mortgaged to the hilt.

Being a nobleman, he was seen as a good catch for marriage and it appears that he was married to a beautiful young woman, who, it seems, had a mind of her own. He often left her alone to carouse with his friends at cockfights in Ballymena and possibly due to his lack of interest in her she turned to another man for love.

He returned early one dark and stormy night accompanied by his drunken friends and rushed upstairs where his wife was entertaining her lover. Enraged by her wantonness he demanded that she stand up and greet his friends. Calmly she refused and cursing her he grabbed a shovel, filled it with red-hot coals from the fire and tossed the burning embers onto her lap.

'Will you rise now?' he demanded.

She did rise and marched out, never to return to Crebilly. When Henry was left on his own, his gambling and high living increased. Determined to put on a show he rebuilt the castle, added a stable block and opened a stud farm and opened a pack of hounds. The kennels for the hounds was built near the bridge, which became known as Kennel Bridge.

The estate was eventually sold and Henry Hamilton O'Hara left to find lowly work as a stable hand in England where his drunkenness caught up with him. When he died of liver disease his body was brought back to be buried in the graveyard of Ballymarlow, a townland near his ancestral home of Crebilly. It is here that the stories of the hauntings abound. It is said that it is his anger at being deprived of his home that raises his spirit each Christmas Eve. He saddles his favourite white mare to gallop the road between the graveyard and the white gates of Crebilly Estate and then to Kennel Bridge, which he leaps over in wild abandon.

Henry Hamilton's column in Ballymarlow graveyard.

have vengeance in this life or the next. He rushed out of the house, jumped on his horse and rode down the laneway at speed. Too late he noticed that the gates were closed, yet he spurred his horse on to make the jump but the horse did not jump high enough. Its front legs caught on the spikes along the top of the white gates and Squire O'Hara was thrown on top of the spikes and decapitated. He died instantly and a few days later was buried at Ballymarlow. A stone column with a sculptured likeness of the squire on top marked his grave. Strangely, it too suffered decapitation when a bolt of lightening struck the head of the column during a terrible storm on the same night of his interment.

Locals say that there is wealth waiting to be discovered in the basement of the mansion but its location is unknown. However, the ghost of the squire haunts the road to dissuade any foolhardy looters from disturbing the land.

There are rumours also of ghostly hooves cantering along the road that would 'make your hair stand on end and if you are wise you'll not stand in the path of the last squire of Crebilly for he's intent on getting his own back'.

(From an article by Dr Robert Simpson for *Belfast Newsletter*, 5 November 1960.)

Another version of the story is that O'Hara was so blinded by fury when he saw his wife in the arms of his best friend that he tore downstairs, cursing them to hell and vowing that he would

5

OMINOUS SIGNS

The Black Nun of Bonamargy

Near Ballycastle on the Cushendall Road stand the windswept ruins of Bonamargy Friary, reputedly the home of the ghost of Sister Julia McQuillan, known locally as 'the Black Nun'.

Rory McQuillan built the friary for the Third Order of Franciscans in 1485 but the MacDonnells later occupied it. Sorley Boy MacDonnell, the most flamboyant of the clan, was responsible for its greatest disaster when he attacked the English forces who were occupying the monastery under Sir John Perrot in 1584 and set fire to the roof. Fortunately, one of the more devout members of the clan set about repairing it right away.

When Sorley Boy died at the great age of 85 in 1590 he was laid to rest in Bonamargy Graveyard beside the friary among the bodies of his kinsmen who were put to death by the sword in Rathlin by the Earl of Essex's troops.

According to a local legend, so many graves were in that burial ground that the earth was a red as newly tilled soil. Perhaps this was the reason why a woman of great piety spent her time praying in the precincts of the friary. Her name was

Sheelah Dubh ni Vilore or Black Julia McQuillan, commonly known as 'the Black Nun of Bonamargy' (the mouth of the Margy River). She was by nature a proud woman, prone to extravagant outbursts of rage if anyone crossed her, but she was also a recluse who practised a severe and gruelling devotion to prayer and was believed to have the gift of prophecy. Several of her predictions have been verified and others are reputedly being fulfilled even yet.

Seven of her more famous prophecies are:

1. Boats would be made of iron.
2. Knocklayde Mountain would burst and the water flowing from it would flood the land for 7 miles around.
3. Two standing stones of Carnduff and Barnish would come together (as they have done in the building of Ballycastle Harbour).
4. Ireland would become independent with the arrival of a sailing ship with her sails on fire.
5. A red-haired cleric from far away would meet his end after saying Mass at Murlock. (In the twentieth century, red-haired Father James McCann drowned

whilst swimming off Pan's rock after saying Mass at Murlock.)

6. The Hilltown River would flow with blood.

7. The time would come when we wouldn't know the difference between winter and summer except for the leaves on the trees.

The story that is told about Julia's conversion to compassion concerns her sister, who lived a sinful and dissolute life, at least by Julia's high moral standards. Her sister was an outcast from the sanctuary and when she became ill and arrived at the abbey door begging for mercy and forgiveness, Sister Julia closed her ears to her cries. However, it was a wild and stormy winter's night and Julia finally relented and allowed her repentant sister to stay in one of the cells. Julia was not of a mind to stay under the same roof as the 'sinner'.

Instead, even though the night was cold and dark, she ventured out into the courtyard to continue with her devotional prayers. She had a strange premonition and something made her glance towards the corner of the courtyard. To her astonishment she saw a mysterious light glimmering outside the window of the cell in which her sister lay. It hovered then floated toward the abbey's doorway and disappeared into the dark interior.

Flustered and shaken, Julia ran into the building and followed in the wake of the light. She sped up the stone steps to the cells. When she arrived at the top the light guided her to the cell where her ill sister lay. The light remained suspended above the bed, shining brightly on her sister's pale face. Once more the girl stretched out her hand and asked for forgiveness from Julia and her God. Holding her hand Julia waited with her until she took her last breath.

At that very second the light vanished and the room became dark. The Black Nun received this as a sign from heaven that her sister had been pardoned. From then on Julia McQuillan endeavoured to be more merciful in judging and more Christian-like in forgiving.

She spent the rest of her life doing good for others and requested that when she died she would be buried without a coffin beneath the entrance to that sacred place so that she might be trodden over by the feet of those who entered. A worn, perforated Celtic cross marks her grave at the west end of the main church.

The local legend holds if you walk around Julia's grave seven times clockwise,

The Black Nun's grave lies underneath the cross.

The Black Nun's likeness.

seven times anti-clockwise and then place your hand through the hole in the cross, you will summon her ghost.

There are several reports of the friary being haunted by the Black Nun's ghost. One report was of a nun running across to the entrance where the stone stairs were, just as Julia did when she followed the light. It is also said that the Black Nun was murdered on these steps leading to the upper floor of the Friary.

Another story tells of a family who entered a dark vaulted passageway when a 2-foot-wide stone seemed to jump out of a wall above them and splinter into pieces just in front of them. An official said that it was almost as if the stone had been pushed out from behind; there was simply no explanation.

A group of people stated that they saw a nun dressed in a habit at a window in the gable wall. She had 'a pale luminescent face and dark eyes and although she was moving she made no sound. The apparition was silent. Deadly silent.'

Galloper Thompson and the Haunting of Jennymount

'The ghost of Galloper Thompson rides recklessly through Belfast on his white horse, scattering people who dare stand in his way until he suddenly disappears

Jennymount Mill.

into nothingness', or so the legend goes.

According to the locals of Mountcollyer Street, Alexandra Park Avenue, Limestone Road and the Grove area, his ghost has been seen frequently, and although these sightings have diminished since the 1900s, many wild and weird happenings are still said to be the work of Galloper.

This area used to be the Jennymount Estate and was owned by the very well-to-do Thompson family who, in the eighteenth and nineteenth centuries, also owned the nearby Jennymount Mill at Milewater. Gordon 'Galloper' Thompson often rode at breakneck speed from his home to the mill and this was the nickname given to him by his employees and servants.

After Thompson's death this devil-may-care behaviour would account for the stories of the rider and his ghostly horse speeding along Jennymount Avenue. It is said that the horse foamed at the mouth and that sweat flew in droplets on passers-by, such was the frenzied riding.

Knowing that he would be the heir to the family's wealth, Galloper Thompson lived a life of dissipation and in his late twenties his waywardness, the drinking and gambling finally caught up with him and he fell desperately ill. His family was warned that he would most probably die but, if he recovered, he undoubtedly would need to change his ways. Unfortunately he became weaker and as the family gathered around his deathbed they begged him to prepare to meet his God.

Had he had the energy he would have laughed at their request but he roused himself enough to declare that he would 'rather have his horse and Jennymount than the highest seat in heaven'. This was blasphemy as far as his family was concerned, but knowing he was dying they faithfully remained at his bedside.

He beckoned his favourite niece to him and whispered a request that he not be buried, but placed somewhere where he would be free to ride his white horse. Some sources say that he asked his niece to kiss him goodbye but when she bent over him and his lips touched her cheek she screamed in agony. The kiss of death left her scarred and marked for life.

With his last breath he gasped, 'Jennymount, Jennymount, how can I leave you?'

His wish to be left where his spirit could roam free was not one that the family wanted to grant so he was taken to the graveyard and it is said that an eerie blue aura surrounded the hearse on its way to his resting place.

But Galloper Thompson did not rest easy in his grave and local people began to whisper that they had seen his headless ghost, especially around Crosscollyer Street, and they even reported hearing the sound of a horse's hooves as he galloped over the little wooden bridge between that street and Seaview Street.

Several versions of the story of Galloper's ghost hold that he told his friends that if he did not find a place in heaven he would return to haunt his beloved Jennymount and ride a horse where he willed.

When one woman in the area came home, almost incoherent with fear and started telling her husband about seeing Thompson's ghost wildly riding a horse on the Limestone Road, the man decided to prove that it was his wife's imagination. He went to the Jennymount stables, where he found that every stall was empty until he reached the last one. As he approached he heard the heavy rasping breathing of an exhausted animal. To his horror he saw it was Thompson's horse covered in a sweaty lather with wild eyes rolling in its head.

We must presume that although Thompson's body lies in its grave his spirit broke free to return and haunt Jennymount as he'd promised.

The members of the family were appalled that they could not be left in peace and after a search they found a minister who would exorcise the ghost of their restless relative.

Apparently the clergyman sealed the spirit in a glass jar, which was to be left undisturbed in the cellar of Jennymount. The family followed the minister's instructions and all was peaceful until one day a maid, who was searching for something in the cellar, came upon the jar and lifted it. Whatever she saw inside terrified her and she dropped the glass, which broke into smithereens. With a flash and a jubilant screech the spirit escaped.

The minister came again and repeated the exorcism but this time the glass was given to a sailor who was asked to take it out to sea, weigh it down and throw it into the depths of the ocean. He was handsomely paid to cast the spirit into the depths, but ... Did he? Is it safely there or has it since resurfaced?

James Haddock's Ghostly Fight for Justice

In the *Ulster Journal of Archaeology*, Volume 3 (1885), author W. Pinkerton wrote:

> At Michaelmass, 1662, Francis Taverner, about 25 years old, a lusty, proper, stout, tall fellow, then a servant at large (afterwards) porter to the Lord Chichester, Earl of Donegall, at Belfast in the North of Ireland, County of Antrim and Diocese of Conor, riding home late one night from Hillsborough, near Drum-bridge, his horse, though of good metal, suddenly made a stand; and

James Haddock's tombstone, c.1657, Drumbeg Churchyard.

he, supposing him to be taken with the staggers, alighted to blood him at the mouth and presently mounted again. As he was setting forward, there seemed to pass by him two horsemen, though he could not hear the treading of their feet, which amazed him. Presently, there appeared a third in a white coat, just at his elbow, in the likeness of James Haddock, formerly an inhabitant in Malone, where he died five years before. Whereupon Taverner asked him, in the name of God, who he was? He replied, I am James Haddock, and you may call to mind by this token that about five years ago, I and two other friends were at your father's house, and you, by your father's appointment, brought us some nuts; and therefore be not afraid, says the apparition.

Taverner remembered the incident and with some courage asked why Haddock appeared to him. He received the reply that Haddock believed him to be a resolute man. The ghost further went on to say that he would give an explanation as to what he wanted him to do.

Tavener refused, and at that moment the air was filled with a cold, clammy feeling. With that, he wheeled his horse about and rode off homeward. Immediately a mighty wind arose and behind him he heard hideous screeches and noises that chilled him. His horse took off and Taverner gave him rein. With a great sense of relief he arrived safely home just as he heard the cock's crow. He fell to his knees in thanksgiving and uttered a prayer. Little did he know that even more horrifying things were yet to come.

The following night the spectre of James Haddock appeared again to him and bid him go to his wife Eleanor who had married a man called Davis after Haddock's death. James and Eleanor had an only son to whom James had given a lease in his will, which he held from Lord Chichester. Davis, by some legal shenanigans, had deprived James and Eleanor's son of his heritage.

Haddock pleaded with Taverner to go to Malone where she lived with Davis and ask her if her maiden name was not Eleanor Welsh; and, 'if it were, to tell her that it was the will of her former husband, James Haddock, that their son should be righted in the lease.'

But Taverner, remembering the strange feeling that had come over him the previous night and the mouldy smell of the grave that emanated from Haddock's ghostly form, could not bring himself do what Haddock asked. He was loath to be seen as deluded by his neighbours.

After a month of nightly visits by the apparition with the spectre becoming even more gruesome, he was eventually persuaded by his wife to go to Malone to see Davis's wife. Although Mrs Taverner could not see the ghost she was well aware of the effect its appearance had on her husband, each time leaving him trembling and pale.

When he finally came face to face with Davis's wife he asked her if her maiden name was Eleanor Welsh and if it was, he had something to say to her. Rather haughtily she replied there was another Eleanor Welsh besides her. Hearing this, Taverner did not deliver his message and he was shown to the door.

However, that very same night as he slept in his bed, he was awakened by something pressing upon him and he saw again the apparition of

James Haddock, who asked him if he had delivered his message. When he answered that he had, the apparition bid him not be afraid before vanishing in a flash of brightness.

Some nights after that appearance Haddock's ghost came again, accused Taverner of not delivering the message and threatened to tear him to pieces if he did not do it. Taverner fled to the home of his friend Pierce, a shoemaker in Belfast, where two of Lord Chichester's servants were also visiting. When they heard the reason for Taverner's distress they prepared to sit up all night to see or hear the spirit that had been torturing him. About midnight, as they were all sitting by the fireside, they watched Taverner's face begin to change and his body being shaken by a terrible trembling.

Francis Taverner watched the apparition materialise opposite where he sat. Taking his courage in hand he held up a candle, moved forward and demanded to know why in God's name it was haunting him. Haddock's ghost replied it was because he had not delivered the message and he threatened again that if this was not done speedily he would make good his promise to tear Taverner to pieces. The ghost changed itself into strange and horrible shapes before vanishing in a white mist.

A dejected and troubled Francis Taverner went to Lord Chichester's house the next day and tearfully told some of the family the reason for the condition he was in. They related the whole sad story to Lord Chichester's chaplain, James South, who then visited Taverner and advised him to go to Malone to deliver his message. Seeing how frightened the man was, he promised to go along with him, although first he wanted to acquaint Dr Lewis Downes, the then minister of

Belfast, about the matter.

It was commonly known by people that Haddock's son had been wronged so Downes went with them to Davis's house in Malone. When Taverner told the woman that the ghost of her former husband, James Haddock, threatened to tear him to pieces if he did not pass on the message, she listened. He related that Davis, her present husband, had wronged her son by changing the lease for Davis's own son to inherit instead of hers and Haddock's. Taverner added that her late husband demanded that she rectify the situation. Immediately he felt calmer and with a peaceful mind thanked James South and Lewis Downes for accompanying him.

About two nights after, the ghost appeared to him again and asked if he had delivered the message. When he answered that he had, Haddock gave him a further task – he must deliver the message to the executors also so that the matter might be settled.

This frightened Taverner, who had assumed that the apparitions of the ghost were finished. He asked the spirit if Davis would try to harm him for bringing the matter to light but he was reassured that Davis would suffer if he attempted anything. With that Haddock once again vanished in a white mist.

The following day Dr Jeremiah Taylor, the Bishop of Down, Connor and Dromore, who presided at the court at Dromore, commanded Taverner to meet him there. He questioned Taverner and was satisfied by the account given to him by Taverner and others that the apparition was true and real.

Dr Taylor advised him to ask these questions the next time the spirit appeared:

Whence are you? Are you a good or a bad spirit? Where is your abode? What station do you hold? How are you regimented in the other world? And what is the reason that you appear for the relief of your son in so small a matter, when so many widows and orphans are oppressed in the world being defrauded of greater matters, and none from thence of their relations appear, as you do, to right them?

That night the bishop sent Taverner to Lord Conway, who was a mentor and friend, in the hope that the ghost would appear. At nine or ten o'clock as he stood by the fireside with his brother and the others who had gathered, his whole countenance changed and he began to tremble, as was usual when the apparition happened. He ran out to the courtyard, followed by his brother, and watched the spirit materialise before him. When it asked Taverner if he had given his messages to the executors also, he replied that he had and wondered if it would still haunt him. 'You need not fear,' replied the ghost. 'You have done what I asked. It is now up to the executor to see that my son receives his inheritance.'

Taverner asked the spirit the questions that the bishop had requested he ask. There was no answer – instead, the spirit crawled slowly over the wall again.

Davis refused to comply with the demands of 'the ghost' and when he met Taverner he scoffed at him and asked what was the use of him being brought to trial when there were no witnesses. When the ghost appeared to Taverner again he urged him to make sure that the case went to trial. Taverner repeated what Davis had said.

'Never mind,' said the ghost, 'I will be present and appear when called upon.'

Taverner reluctantly consented. The trial came on at Carrickfergus and, needless to say, there was much speculation.

The opposing counsel browbeat and upbraided Taverner for inventing an absurd and malicious story against his neighbour Davis about the lease, and ended up by tauntingly desiring him to call his witness. The Usher of the Court, with a sceptical sneer, called upon 'James Haddock' and at a third repetition of the name, a clap of thunder shook the court house to its foundation; a hand was seen upon the witness bible. And a voice was heard saying: 'Is this enough?'

Naturally the terrified jury were at one in giving a verdict in favour of young Haddock. Davis, amid the execration of the crowd slunk away from court and on his way home fell off his horse and broke his neck.

That same evening Francis Taverner had his last visit from the ghost who warmly thanked him for his services. But Taverner's curiosity overcame him and he asked if Haddock was happy in the 'other world'. The ghost answered him, 'If you were not the man you are, I would tear you to pieces for daring to ask such a question.'

With that the ghost swept off in a flash of fire and Taverner never saw him again. However, when the story of James Haddock's appearances circulated around the countryside, people were loath to meet him. So, in order to make sure that he did not escape from his unearthly existence again, his headstone was upended and tumbled across his grave in

'Is this enough?'

the belief that his ghost could not push it aside.

And so it lies in that position to this day.

These facts were all authenticated by Thomas Alcock, secretary to Bishop Jeremy Taylor, who recorded the whole affair in choice Latin.

The Witch of Glentow

Glentaisie is one of the smallest of glens of Antrim and it takes its name from a princess who fled from Rathlin Island after a great battle. This glen is also known in the anglicised form as Glentow and that is the name that is associated with a woman who was known as 'the Witch of Glentow'.

It is said that her name was McDade and she was born in the 1860s. She was a lone and solitary woman, who dressed in black clothes and wore a bonnet, as was the style in those days. When she came to Glentaisie she made her home in an old abandoned sheep shelter in the Hanging Wood on the slope at Bromore and near the two raths of Bromore and Crookabroom.

Local people were puzzled by her arrival there and it must be said that her dour demeanour raised their suspicions. She begged for food and would sit by the river to eat, after which she generally fell asleep. Some people were more generous than others, and about 2 years after she came to Glentaisie the woman went to the door of a local farmer called Graham, whose wife was always kind to her. On that particular day Mrs Graham was in a foul mood and told the old woman to be off, she would give her nothing. But the woman continued to beg in a whining voice and the farmer's wife struck her on the face and warned her never to return. When the old woman left, Mrs Graham had a fit of remorse and tried to call her back but she was nowhere to be seen. The next morning Mrs Graham took her pail and went to milk two of her best cows but they had mysteriously ceased yielding, even though there was no sign of anything wrong with them.

She hurried upstairs to tell her husband but he wasn't in any mood to listen. He had his own worries, he told her. The previous day he'd been to the market in Ballymoney and sold a cow. He met two friends from Armoy and they celebrated the sale together. Unfortunately, a thief heard him boasting of the great price he'd got and when he was tipsy his money was stolen.

Mrs Graham was distraught because the half-yearly rent was almost due and she had nowhere to turn for the money. Was this her punishment for her lack of generosity the previous day?

A few weeks after this event a farmer from nearby Carnsampson accused the old woman of stealing potatoes from his field. When she protested her innocence he cursed her as a thief and a liar. The next morning two of the man's sheep were gone. A few days later they were found slaughtered near the old sheep shelter and the rumour spread like quick-fire that the old woman was a witch who wreaked vengeance on anyone who crossed her. From then on she was labelled 'the Witch of Glentow' and terror came to every household in the area.

After that, when other strange things began to happen in the area, the witch was considered to be responsible. One young lad who lived in Hillhead saw her passing his home and he threw some stones at her, one of which caused her head to bleed. She hurried off muttering under her breath and the next day he was found lying in a field with a cut on his forehead in the exact same place as the cut on the old woman. We can only imagine how folk shuddered in fear and horror when the old woman passed by. People cast their eyes down in case they would be the next to suffer from her evil magic.

The story goes that three reckless young men from Ballycastle planned to teach her a lesson in the hope that they would drive her away. Filled with bravado on the night of the Auld Lammas Fair they waited for her on the road near the limestone quarry at Milltown and, grabbing her, carried her off to the local quarry. All the while she cursed and screamed but they laughed and without mercy threw her over the precipice. Then they tore her bag to shreds and threw it over the edge after her, and hearing no sound walked away. Believing that workmen would find her in the morning and assume she had fallen over the edge, they decided to keep what they had done a secret. Yet, the men congratulated themselves presuming that if she was indeed alive then their action had scared her off.

For almost a year no one saw or heard of the witch and people began to breathe freely again, but quite regularly a strange sound came from the Hanging Wood on

Bromore slope. Then on the day of the following Lammas Fair, the old witch reappeared, wearing the same clothes and carrying the same bag, apparently untorn. She looked balefully at each person who passed but spoke not one word. People wondered what she lived on because she no longer begged. Yet, occasionally, inexplicable things happened which were attributed to her evil enchantment.

And it was no surprise that the three young men lived in a state of anxiety, waiting for her evil spell to befall them. So, rather than wait, they decided to take action. On New Year's Eve they crept to her hut, but one of the young men sprained his foot on the rocky ground. However, the other two lured her outside, gagged her, then carried her for over 2 miles to the shore, where they flung her into the sea at the little port.

As soon as the old woman's body touched the water a huge wave arose and almost pulled them into the tide. Then, as they waded out of the water, they heard an unearthly wail. A yellow light flashed above them and a wraith in white appeared and floated towards the nearby glen. Unsurprisingly, in a state of blind panic, they rushed to their homes.

Next day they related the story to their friends, still shaken by the horrendous and fearsome sight they had encountered the previous night. When nothing happened during the next weeks they relaxed and regained their good humour but on Candlemas Day, 2 February at midnight, the two young men were found lying dead in their beds with a strange mark on their chests. It was circular with spokes representing a wheel with one spoke missing. Lying on the floor was a piece of paper with the exact same marking. No one could explain the deaths or the markings.

At Easter the same year a girl from Glendun was visiting her friend in Ballycastle and heard the story. She mentioned that there was a spaewife (fortune-teller or prophetess) in her glen who could possibly explain the riddle of the markings. A gift of money and a bottle of poteen had to be presented, so the two girls went to the spaewife who invited them to sit down. They mentioned the strange death of the two lads, but before saying anything about the strange markings on their bodies the spaewife took a stick and drew an exact copy of the symbol of a wheel with a broken rim.

The woman demanded the two pieces of paper and then asked the girls to leave the house. She slammed the door shut and then darkened the windows as the girls listened outside. The Ballycastle girl was sure that she heard the voice of another person, which resembled that of the old witch.

After some minutes the door opened and the spaewife motioned them inside. She said that the two men had murdered the old woman and the spoke missing on the circular marking meant a vacant chair in each home. As the girls rose to leave she added something else – the name of the third person who set out to harm the witch that night but who was not present at the final act. Because of that he would live another 10 years but he would suffer greatly from festering boils. This young man suffered and died 10 years to the day after his fellow conspirators.

A verse in those parts well recalls that strange old woman:

So now after nightfall her voice they
    can hear,
Her eerie moans filling the bosom

with fear,
By the side of the water she wanders
somehow,
Where you'll hear the dread cry of the
Witch of Glentow.

The Cow Herder and the Ghost

David Hunter, a cow herder for the Bishop of Down and Conor, lived near Portmore Lough in south-west County Antrim. He was carrying a log into the dairy when a strange apparition of an old woman materialised before him. She did not resemble anyone he knew and he was so shocked at her sudden appearance that he dropped the log and ran to the house.

His wife was alarmed at the expression she saw on his face, and when he slipped to the floor in a dead faint she was even more puzzled and worried. After she had helped him to bed, she walked outside to check what could have caused the change in him but there was nothing unusual in the barn or the dairy. She returned and bolted the door of the house and when she went into the bedroom her husband was in a deep sleep.

The following night the apparition came back and even before David reached the dairy he felt an overwhelmingly strange seductive power drawing him to her. Such was the weird force she exerted that he followed her every night, all night, for the next 9 months. Whenever she came he had a compulsion to follow her through the woods and beyond. Surprisingly for a woman of her apparent great age she moved very quickly.

It seemed that he was bewitched and he felt that his legs were nearly worn to nothing so tired was he. Even when he was in bed with his wife he had to rise and go if the old woman appeared. In the beginning his wife locked all the doors and windows and tried to hold him inside but she was no match for the power that the spirit held over him.

Reluctant to allow him to be led away on his own each night, she followed and even though she saw nothing herself she walked behind him until daybreak. They had a little dog that showed no fear in the presence of the old woman and even seemed to know the apparition quite well because he faithfully followed his master.

David was confounded one night when he saw the spirit pass right through a tree that stood in her way. Yet he said nothing and walked around the tree and continued to follow her. In all of this time she had never spoken a single word. But one evening as he was going over a hedge onto the road, he came up against her when she stopped without warning. At the contact he cried out in frustration and fear, 'Lord bless me, I wish I was dead! Shall I never be delivered of this misery?'

The woman spoke immediately, in a rasping voice. 'And the Lord bless me too. It was a very happy circumstance that you spoke first, for until then I had no power to speak. That is why I have followed you so long,' she said.

'My name is Margaret, I lived here before the war and had one son by my husband. When he died I married a soldier, by whom I had several children, whom my son maintained, else we must all have starved. He lives beyond Bann water. Pray go to him and bid him dig under the hearth and there he shall find 28 shillings. Let him pay what I owe

Her spirit passed right through a tree.

to the minister and the rest to the charge unpaid at my funeral.'

She handed David a note with the name of the church written down. David refused to do what the old woman asked but she began to wail and lament and his wife, who was standing close by, heard her husband arguing with her. She still could not see anyone but when he began to rant and rave and cry out, 'No', several times, she prayed that whatever was causing his distress would lift the burden from him.

The old woman was crying so bitterly that eventually he felt compelled to do as she asked. When he agreed, she vanished almost immediately and the night was filled with the sweet sound of music.

David's wife brought him home and the next morning they set out for the Bann water to carry out the request, and never again was he troubled by the frightening appearance of that ghostly old woman.

The Ghosts of Rathlin

Rathlin Island is the only inhabited island off the coast of Northern Ireland and it has one of the goriest, most murderous and haunted histories in Ireland.

Although there is evidence that people lived there as long as 8,000 years ago, it must have been a more fertile place then, because much of it is inhospitable and bare these days. Yet it has a wild beauty and when the high sheer cliffs along the coast are battered by the waves of the North Atlantic one can easily understand why there is a large number of caves. Many of these are inaccessible by land and can only be reached by boat but it is known that several of them penetrate deep into the cliffs.

Some dark stories are told of these caves. One of the worst recorded was the massacre in the year 1575 of over 400 old men, women and children.

Chieftan Sorley Boy McDonnell had sent them to hide in the caves while he set off to the mainland to fight the English troops. However, he spied the enemy ships of Sir Francis Drake, with Colonel John Norreys in command, sailing towards the island. As he watched helplessly from the mainland all he could do was to pray that his wife and children would be safe.

The English managed to land and storm the castle on Rathlin and although it was against the rules of siege warfare they killed the Scottish troops who were based there. Of the servants and women housed in the castle, about 200 in all died by the sword. On Norrey's order his troops then descended to the caves and slaughtered the 400 fugitives hiding there. No mercy was shown – they even tore children from their mothers' arms and murdered them. It is said that the screams of the victims could be heard echoing across the water all the way to the mainland and that the rocks were so stained with blood that the tide could not erase the evidence of the butchering.

'They were hunted as if they had been seals or otters and all destroyed.' So it was reported by George Hartwig in *The Subterranean World*, published in 1871. It was said that Lord Essex, the English deputy and overall commander, wrote to Queen Elizabeth I, 'that Sorley Boy, from the mainland saw the taking of the island and was likely to have run mad for sorrow, tearing and tormenting himself and saying that he there lost all that he ever had.'

To this very day the caves are said to echo with the wails of the ghosts of those who were murdered.

The Ghost of Cooraghy

On the west of Rathlin there is a remote bay called Cooraghy. One evening when the fish were running, three fishermen cast their lines and such was their success that they forgot the time. With the fading light they decided that it would be safer to stay the night in one of the caves.

They gathered their gear and entered the nearest cave where they found a flat-topped rock that neatly served as a table. Collecting some driftwood they lit a fire and brewed their tea chatting all the while about the good day's fishing.

Soon the tea was ready and they placed their three mugs on the flat rock. Suddenly a hand shot out of the gloom and placed a fourth mug on the boulder. Not paying much attention, they filled the mug without looking to see who owned it. It was only when the hand shot out again to take the mug that they looked and realised that they were not alone.

It's no surprise to hear that they bolted and later were told that the hand belonged to the devil himself. Truth to tell the terrified fishermen never went back to retrieve their mugs!

The Wraith of Rathlin

The people of Rathlin Island (Rackery) were well used to saying goodbye to folk emigrating to America, for it was hard enough to make a living on the island. Often they would gather near the West Lighthouse to catch one last glimpse of the emigrant ship as it sailed away.

The emigrants and their families knew that they would probably never see each other again and the pain of parting was almost unbearable. Yet some strange stories told on the island suggest that the connection to home could not be broken.

There was a man called Joe McCurdy who had a farm in Cabbal, a place not far from the lighthouse. In those days, farmers helped each other out and if something needed doing there was an exchange of labourers. It was a good system because any farmer could be sure of help when he needed it.

When Joe was a child of about 7 years old, his father Joseph was building a new stable with the help of neighbours and Joe, being a curious child, went out to have a look at it. When he went into the stable there was a man on his knees praying, the rosary beads slipping through his fingers in the same way that his father's did. The man was so deep in prayer that he didn't notice the boy.

Even though he was quite young, Joe thought it a bit strange that a man would be kneeling in the stable praying, so he went back into the house to tell his mother. The men were sitting at the kitchen table eating and Joe became a bit excited telling his mother about it so she sent the men out to see who the strange man was. But they could find no sign of him and came back to question Joe further.

'What did he look like? What was he wearing?'

All Joe could tell them was that the man was wearing a funny-looking coat and that he was praying on his beads. Determined to get to the bottom of the story, for they recognised that there was a ring of truth about it, they sent for Michael Black who was known to be good at interpreting signs like this.

Michael was a big strong man but when Joe told him about the man in the stable, he began to cry. He started to rock forward and back and through his tears he cried out, 'That was our Laughlin who's dead and gone to heaven. Our poor wee Laughlin Veg who went away to America.'

Now that wraith's appearance was an unusual happening but not an unbelievable one. The woman took note of the date and barely 3 months afterwards the islanders heard that Laughlin had indeed died on the date when his wraith had come back to appear on his island home.

6

PERSONAL STORIES

OFTEN when I research stories and interview people, unexpected things come to light and the idea of a 'time slip' is one. This could perhaps be explained by the existence of a 'fourth dimension' or simply by a moment when the past becomes a reality in the present.

Heather Barclay related the following story of an incident that she and others experienced near Larne.

Time Slip at Doagh

'There were six of us in the car on our way home from a dance in McConnell's in Doagh. It was about half one or maybe two o'clock in the morning. It was just past the pig farm on the left-hand side of the road where it widens out but as we were coming towards the narrow bit –that's where we saw them, on the old road. There was a big herd of horses, about fifteen to twenty of them galloping along full belt. They were actually heading for our car. They all seemed to be white with their tails flying out behind them.

Robert's theory is that it was a time slip; they had crossed into our dimension on the old Irish Highway. The horses were galloping along in their time and just crossed over to our time for a split second. I began to call out to the fella, who was driving, and I just got out the words, 'Watch those hor ...' and they disappeared – vanished, before I even finished the word.

The white horses at Doagh.

I've never seen them since, but coming along there at night I always think of them and I get a rare feeling, but because it was horses they weren't scary for us – it was the strangest thing but all of us saw them. It wasn't our imagination.

Haunted House outside Carrickfergus

Heather told me another story that happened in her sister's house, but she was not afraid of the presence of ghosts there because they were benign. To her mind they were just traces of energy left behind by people who had once lived in the house.

My brother-in-law worked for the Water Board and they all had houses that went with the job. My sister lived in the old water commissioner's house at the dam about 2 miles outside of Carrickfergus. It was well over 100 years old and it was definitely haunted.

Some strange things happened, but my sister wasn't in the least frightened. She just accepted the haunting as part of the house's history. One night she heard singing and she saw a lady in the room polishing the furniture. She was singing something to the air of 'Amazing Grace' but it was different words. My sister said that she had no sense of fear and the woman, taking no notice of her, went on polishing as if she wasn't there. After a few moments the ghost just disappeared.

One day I was sitting in the kitchen having a cup of tea with my sister, when just out of nowhere we could smell pipe tobacco. Although we were both smokers at the time, pipe tobacco had a very distinctive smell. We just looked at each other because both of us smelled it at the same time but we didn't see anyone.

One other time she was downstairs alone and she could hear children playing upstairs and doors opening and closing but her own children weren't in.

The Water Board sold off the house and my sister and her husband bought it. All in all they lived there for over 20 years. My sister loved the house, ghosts and all.

Belfast Wraith

A crisis apparition is a ghost or spirit that appears within 12 hours of a person's death either before or after it has taken place … They appear to communicate their death or their impending death to a loved one. Some indicate that they have been injured, others are simply reassuring or request the assistance of a loved one. (Hurrel & Lewis)
[A wraith is a crisis communication.]

My mother-in-law lived in Belfast and her father took ill so her mother did most of the work. One evening she heard a loud knocking at the door and when she opened it her mother's wraith came in past her and walked up the stairs. My mother-in-law was not a fanciful person but when she experienced that she did not doubt it. Her mother had died quite suddenly from a heart problem, although she was quite a young age.

BIBLIOGRAPHY

Arlincourt, C.V.P., *The Three Kingdoms: England, Scotland, Ireland. 1844* (reprinted by Royal Society of Antiquaries of Ireland. Dublin. 1905)

Baker, J., *Haunted Belfast* (Nonsuch Publishing. Dublin. 2007)

Baker, J. & Liggett, M., *Ulster Ghost Stories*. Historical Belfast Special Edition. (Glenravel Local History Project. 1994. Belfast)

Belanger, J. *The World's Most Haunted Places* (Career Press. Wayne, NJ. 2004)

Byrne, P.F., *Irish Ghost Stories* (Mercier: Cork. 1965)

Byrne, P.F., *Tales of the Banshee* (Mercier. Cork. 1987)

Campbell, M., *Long Ago Tales of Rathlin Island* (J.S. Scarlett & Son. 1964)

Coghlan, R., *A Dictionary of Irish Myth and Legend* (Donard Publishing Company. 1979)

Cooper Foster, J., *Ulster Folklore* (H.R. Carter Publications Ltd. Belfast. 1951)

Corcorran, J.A., *Irish Ghosts* (Geddes & Grosset, Scotland. 2001)

Craik, D., *Unknown Country* (MacMillan & Co. London 1887)

Curran, B., *A Bewitched Land* (The O'Brien Press. Dublin. 2008)

Curran, B., *Beasts, Banshees and Brides from the Sea*. (Appletree Press Ltd. Belfast. 1996)

Danaher, K., *Folktales of the Irish Countryside*. (Mercier Press, Cork. 1967)

Dublin Penny Journal, Vol. 3 & 4 (Dublin. 1835)

Dunne, J.J., *Haunted Ireland*. (Appletree Press, Belfast. 1977)

Evans, E.E., *Irish Folkways*. (Routledge & Keegan Paul, London. 1972)

Frazer, J.G., *The Golden Bough*. (McMillan & Co. London. 1894)

Gregory, Lady, *Complete Irish Mythology* (Octopus Publishing Group, London. 1994)

Hardy, P.D., *The northern tourist, or, Stranger's guide to the North and North-west of Ireland* (W. Curry. Dublin. 1830)

Hayward, R., *In praise of Ulster* (Arthur Barker, London. 1938)

Hurrel, J. & Lewis, R.L., *The Unexplained: A Sour Book*. (Flame Tree Publishing London. 2003)

Jenkins, J.L., *Black Magic and Bogeymen* (Cork University Press. Cork. 2014)

Journal of the Royal Society of Antiquaries of Ireland. 9 (RSA London. 1890)

Lysaght, P., *The Banshee*. (O'Biren Press, Dublin. 1986)

Mason, W.S., *A Statistical Account, or, Parochial Sur of Ireland: Drawn Up ...*, Vol. 2 (Graisberry and Campbell, Dublin. 1816)

McCahan, R, *History of Rathlin Island* (The Glex of Antrim Historical Society, Coleraine. 192: reprinted 1988)

McCahan, R., *The Giant's Causeway and Dunluce C* (Antrim Historical Society, Coleraine. 1988)

Murphy. M.J., *Rathlin: Island of Blood and Enchantment* (Dundalgan Press (W. Tempest) Dundalk. 1987)

Reed, T., *Travels in Ireland in the Year 1822* (Long Hurst, Rees, Orme & Brown. London. 1829)

Scott, M., *Irish Ghosts and Hauntings* (Warner B GB. 1994)

Seymour, St. John. & Nelligan, H., *True Irish Gl. Stories* (Allen Figgis Ltd. Dublin. 1969)

Sheane, M., *The Glens of Antrim* (A.H. Stockwel Ltd., Ilfracombe, Devon. 2010)

Smith. D.A. *Guide to Irish Mythology*. (Irish Acac Press. Sallins, Kildare. 1988)

Twiss, R.A., *Tour in Ireland in 1775* (Author. London. 1776)

Ulster Journal of Archaeology, Vol. 8, 9 & 17. (Ulst Archaeological Society. Belfast. 1860)

Underwood, P. I., *Irish Ghosts: A Ghost Hunter's Guide* (Amberley Publishing Stroud, Glouc 2012)

Wilde, W.R., *Irish Popular Superstitions* (Irish University Press. Shannon. 1852)